THE STORY OF WILLOW RUN

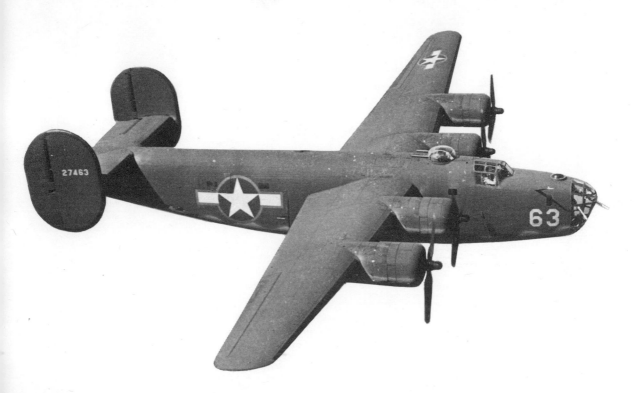

THE STORY

Ann Arbor The University of Michigan Press

OF WILLOW RUN

Marion F. Wilson

PREFACE

To make an educational program suitable to a community requires a basic knowledge of the background and conditions of that community. Usually a community develops slowly from a small beginning and makes adjustments gradually. Willow Run did not follow the normal pattern; rather it was a large community which appeared overnight as a result of a federal housing project. The experiences which come from such a development are likely never to be repeated. Therefore it seemed fitting to gather some of this information while first-hand sources were still available.

The Board of Education authorized Marion Wilson to compile a history of this community with particular emphasis on the period during which Willow Run Village operated as a federal housing project. Miss Wilson has been associated with the operation of the housing project since its beginning. This story will undoubtedly revive memories for some readers, for others it will deepen their understanding, to all it will provide an insight into a type of pioneering which existed during and following World War II.

It was with considerable effort that the story of the beginning of this community has been made available. It is our hope that the readers will enjoy this review of the past, and that the students and local residents will take up the challenge of building a truly democratic community.

Robert Stevenson
Assistant Superintendent, Willow Run Schools

For Emily Case

ACKNOWLEDGMENTS

Robert Stevenson, Assistant Superintendent, and Mrs. Nell Barrett, Head Librarian, of the Willow Run Schools, both felt the need of a local history for reference use in the junior and senior high schools. Since it was permissible to use certain library funds for the writing and promotion of local history, they recommended to the school board that the funds be used for this purpose. The book was written under contract with the Willow Run School Board.

Henry Edmunds, Stanley Graham, and the staff at the Ford Archives at Fairlane in Dearborn made available the necessary research material about the Ford Bomber Plant and provided many of the photographs.

Former public housing staff members at Willow Run who loaned materials and pictures from their personal files were Viola Blackenburg, Dorothy I. Cline, and Francis X. Servaites. Ken Cavanaugh, a former manager of Willow Run, checked official files in Washington for verification of certain basic data. Paul J. Moore, present manager of the project, did the research on budgets, costs, and taxes.

The **Ypsilanti Press** and the **Ann Arbor News,** both of which serve the area, made available their files and provided photographs.

Special thanks are due the many Willow Run "old-timers" who either wrote their stories or gave generously of their time for interviews. What they wrote and said expressed the feelings of many thousands of the people who lived at Willow Run.

Marion F. Wilson

CONTENTS

THE STORY OF WILLOW RUN

PROLOGUE 1

WILLOW RUN . . . "Willow Run," the name. What does it mean?

It's a quiet stream that flows into the Huron River and it's a gracious chapel nearby.

It was a place where Indians camped and hunted and where pioneers cleared the

forest, built their cabins, settled and farmed the land.

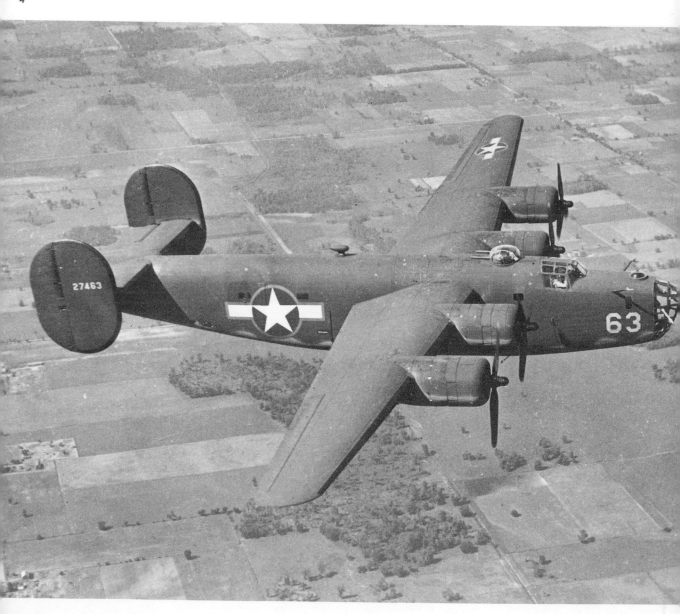

WILLOW RUN . . .

Willow Run was a camp for boys where they learned to farm,

to live in the open, to work and love the land.

The name stands for the giant plant first run by Henry Ford,

where B-24 bombers were built to help gain victories in World War II;

then run by the Kaiser-Frazer Corporation where cars were built and where the

C-119, known as the "Flying Boxcar," was built for the U.S. Army;

now the great plant where the General Motors Corporation builds

hydramatic transmissions for its cars.

WILLOW RUN ...

Willow Run is a fine airport that is known to travelers and pilots around the world.

WILLOW RUN . . .

Willow Run is a community of temporary houses where thousands of the people

lived who built the bombers that helped win the war, where thousands of veterans

who fought to win the war came to live with their wives and children, so that they

could continue war-interrupted educations, the community often being called the

"second campus" of the University of Michigan at Ann Arbor.

WILLOW RUN ...

Willow Run is where every family has a yard where children can play and there are no signs at the rental office saying "No Children Allowed."

WILLOW RUN . . .

Willow Run is a name that sings of pioneers of many kinds, the pioneering people who built the bombers, then built the products of peacetime at the place where people learned to live together in harmony, to go to good schools, to learn to be good citizens of a community of which they could be proud.

WILLOW RUN . . .

Willow Run is not only the place, it is the people, their spirit; the spirit of pioneers.

WILLOW RUN . . . Willow Run is America!

PROLOGUE 2

Once upon a time there was a boy who lived on a Michigan farm in Washtenaw County. It was a Sunday afternoon in early December. He wanted to go out and hunt rabbits.

"No," said his father, "there is not enough snow for good tracking. You would just be wasting your shells."

The boy got his jacket and cap from the hook behind the kitchen door. "Guess I'll just go for a walk, then." As he sauntered toward the barn to call his dog he thought, "What a place. When there were pioneers here like grandpa talks about, things happened."

The boy's dog came running when he whistled. "Nothing ever happens here," he said to the dog. The dog did not seem to mind. He was ready to chase rabbits. The two of them went down the long lane to the edge of the pasture. As they passed by the gate the dog stopped suddenly. He sniffed the air, then, nose to the ground and tail waving, started after a rabbit. The boy, lonesome for his gun, picked up a handful of stones.

"If I see that rabbit," he said, "bet I can hit him with a rock."

The dog raced down the fence-row, then turned and ran to the top of the knoll. He stood there sniffing. The boy raced to the top. He looked down one way, then the other. He could see no rabbit. He ran down to the edge of the small stream and looked across at the quiet chapel.

Then he remembered a Sunday last summer. It had been a bright blue morning. Fluffy clouds, fat and white, had played tag in the sky. Soft organ music had rolled from the chapel, over the stream, and up the bank to him. Today it was gray, the damp air cold and sharp. There was no organ music—only the chill stillness. He sat down on the bank and looked into the cold blue stream. "Willow Run," he said, looking hard at the water. "You are so little they can't even call you a river. Just little Willow Run."

The dog, ashamed of having lost the rabbit, wandered down the bank to the stream. The boy threw a stone into the stream. As it plopped and sank, a circle moved out along the surface of the water.

"Boom!" he said aloud, thinking of his shotgun. He threw another stone nearer the shore. The new circle made a big circle, and a bigger circle. The last reaching circle cracked the thin ice near the bank. "Boom!" said the boy. He threw all of his stones hard at the stream. Many circles moved out, around, and crossed over each other.

"Nothing ever happens here," he said sadly, looking across again at the peaceful chapel on the other side of Willow Run. "Nothing ever happens here at Willow Run."

On the other side of the world something was happening. Enemy planes loaded with bombs sped across the early sky. A group of American ships sat quietly in an American harbor—Pearl Harbor.

The bombs roared in one enormous booming sound. Minutes later many of the American ships were ripped, torn, blown up. The roaring screech of those bombs raced up to the sky, making itself one with the radio waves. The sound sped across the ocean and up over the mountains and valleys, into the towns and cities.

The United States of America had been attacked. The country was at war. The roar from those bombs had repercussions that bounced and circled around the world, like giant rocks thrown into a giant stream. The scream of those bombs made things happen fast in America, made things happen fast at Willow Run—Willow Run, the quiet stream with its peaceful chapel.

What happened to our boy? To our boy who liked pioneers and liked to hunt rabbits, who liked soft organ music from the quiet chapel by the clear blue stream, Willow Run?

Our boy, like thousands of other Americans, became one of the new pioneers—the new pioneers who helped make the name "Willow Run" a roaring sound-circle that boomed around the world.

CAMP WILLOW RUN

1

Henry Ford was a pioneer. He led the way for the mass-production of automobiles. But besides his skill and knowledge in things mechanical, he had a great love of the land. Since Mr. Ford had such a strong feeling for the land, he had purchased several hundred acres at Willow Run in Washtenaw County. He felt that if young men could know the use of the land, the feel of the land and the things it could do, they would be better citizens, better men. Because of this conviction, he sponsored two camps for boys where they could raise crops from the land.

The first camp was near Dearborn and was called "Camp Legion." This first camp was so successful he opened the second camp in 1939 on the banks of the stream, Willow Run. It was called "Camp Willow Run." The boys who were selected for the camps were the sons of veterans of World War I.

The boys at Camp Willow Run lived in army tents. There was a mess hall and a chapel. The sixty-five boys came to the camp in April and stayed until early in November. They farmed the three hundred and twenty acres next to the camp, working eight hours a day for twenty-five cents an hour. Mr. Ford provided the use of the land, the tents, the tractors and equipment; the boys did the work. They raised vegetables and sold them at a stand at one end of the farm, on Ecorse Road. At the end of the season, after the expenses of seed and fertilizer had been paid, plus the cost for the food they did not raise, the profit was divided among the boys.

William Coon, resident of Willow Run Village and a member of the Resident Council, was one of the boys in Camp Willow Run in 1941. "That was a wonderful summer," he told me. "Of course, it was sort of like the army with lots of rules, but we all really loved the work. We were healthy and gained weight. Besides the two dollars a day which I earned—and that was good pay in those days—there was enough profit at the end of the summer which, when divided, gave each of us a hundred and sixty-eight dollars. With what I had saved from my two dollars a day and my season's end profit, I bought my first car."

I asked Bill Coon what kind of a car he had bought. It was a Ford.

The last summer that Camp Willow Run was in operation was 1941. The ground was broken for the Bomber Plant in April of 1941, and enough of the building was finished by that fall so that they were able to begin the manufacture of parts for the famous B-24 Bomber

Another boy who lived and worked at Camp Willow Run was Ted Winters. He lived in Ypsilanti. He loved music; he wanted to study music and to be an engineer.

"He was a wonderful boy," said Mrs. Frances Geiser, a former Ypsilantian who is now married and lives with her husband in Nancy Park in Ypsilanti Township. "I went to high school with Ted. We took piano lessons from the same teacher. He had a great deal of talent."

In the summer of 1940 Ted Winters was one of the boys at Camp Willow Run. Because of his interest and training in music, he played the organ in the chapel at Willow Run for the Sunday services. Ted did not know, when he played the music for these services, that on the other side of the knoll, a huge plant was planned and would be built. He did not know that the little farm boy who listened to his music across the fields and who complained that "nothing ever happens" would see a great new community built just across the way. He did not know that that huge plant would make the famous American bomber, the B-24, known around the world as the "Liberator." When Ted played the organ he did not know this. He just loved to play the organ on Sunday in the chapel by the stream, Willow Run.

When his country was at war, Ted joined the United States Army Air Corps. Because of his interest in engineering, he became a radio operator. He was assigned to a squadron that flew a B-24. In 1943, Ted Winters was killed in a B-24 over the English Channel, far from his beloved chapel. Ted Winters is a local hero. His spirit belongs to Ypsilanti, to Camp Willow Run, to all of us in this community.

WILLOW RUN BEFORE THE VILLAGE

2

Willow Run is a quiet, clear, blue stream which flows into the Huron River. The Huron River flows southeast and into Lake Erie, just below the Detroit River.

In the days of long ago, the land around Willow Run and the Huron River was heavily wooded. This meant plenty of wild game: deer, bear, rabbit, and pheasant. Willow Run was a favorite camping place for the Indians a hundred and fifty years ago. They often pitched their camps on the banks of the stream. Nearby was one of their favorite trails, the Sauk-Fox Trail which led all the way across the state to Lake Michigan. This old Indian trail is now Michigan Avenue, U.S. highway 112.

The early settlers first came to Willow Run in 1823. They built log cabins to live in and cleared a bit of land around the cabins on which to raise a little grain, a few vegetables. They hunted in the woods for their meat.

In spite of the fact that the Michigan Central Railway was laid from Detroit to Ypsilanti in 1838, the Willow Run area was pioneer country. The cabins were scattered, and the Indians came around frequently. This had been the Potawatomies' camping and hunting land for a great many years. The wives of the early settlers were frightened until they learned that the Indians were superstitious. They placed a home-made broom, which was called a besom, crosswise in their doorways, and since the Indians were afraid of a besom, they stayed away.

The new railroad encouraged the lumber business, so as more and more trees were cut down, the country was cleared for farms. For a great many years, Willow Run was a place of good farms. Some of the farmers planted orchards which became rich and plentiful with apples, cherries, and peaches. Most of the families around Willow Run and in Ypsilanti Township were farm families who were not interested in city living. They were very satisfied living on their farms, even though they did not have electricity and indoor plumbing as we have today. They used kerosene lamps and lanterns and got their water from wells.

Professor Lowell Carr, of the University of Michigan, wrote a book called **Willow Run.** In it he tells about talking to Mr. Stedman, a Willow Run old-timer:

"Many a time my father used to fall asleep up in the cabin listening to the wolves howling back in the woods right where the Bomber Plant stands now, and many's the winter morning that he and his two brothers would wake up to find an inch or two of snow dusted across them from chinks in the cabin roof. It was an hour's walk through the woods to Ypsilanti then, and two or three days by ox team to Detroit."

In spite of the wintry winds, the howling of wolves, gradually more and more settlers moved into the area. More timber was cut to build the homes and the land was cleared for farming. For many years to follow, the Willow Run area was a community of large, productive farms, owned by individual families.

The first school in the area to have the name "Willow Run" was a one-room building on Rawsonville Road. It was in the district just east of our present school district, in Washtenaw County near Willow Run Creek. Because of a bend in the road which did not coincide with the dividing line between Wayne County and Washtenaw County, the playground of Willow Run School was located in Wayne County. With the consolidation of rural school districts, the Willow Run School was closed and the children attended the Van Buren Consolidated School in Belleville.

Henry Ford had purchased a great deal of land in the area around the old Willow Run School; in 1931 he purchased the old school, which had been closed, and had it rehabilitated and made into a model of a one-room school. The **Ypsilanti Press** on September 9, 1931, ran a story which stated:

Henry Ford forgot the busy life of a motor magnate for a few hours this morning to watch children troop into Willow Run School, one of the few remaining "little red schoolhouses" of "reading, writin' and 'rithmetic" days.

The building, situated on the Wayne-Washtenaw County Line Road, had been closed since the consolidation of the rural districts to form the Van Buren Consolidated School at Belleville, and was re-opened today after it had been remodeled by Mr. Ford.

Superintendent John Myron of the Van Buren Consolidated School opened the fall term. The program was turned over to Frank Cody, Superintendent of Schools in Detroit. He began his teaching career at the old Willow Run School.

In checking two other newspapers, the **Herald,** a paper published by the students at the Edison Institute, and the **Ford News,** published by the Ford Motor Company, one finds that the old school was completely rehabilitated by Mr. Ford. The desks and tables were of white pine with dowel construction. It was lighted by kerosene lamps and heated by a square box wood stove. We find some modern conveniences for a one-room schoolhouse: The outside toilets had flowing spring water supplied by a dam on the bank of Willow Run Creek, and an electric hot water heater provided hot water for the wash basins.

This Willow Run School under the sponsorship of Henry Ford continued for several years. An average of thirty pupils were enrolled in the first through the eighth grades, which were taught by one teacher, Miss Mackinnon. The janitor for the school not only took care of the building, but also taught woodworking to the boys and served the school lunches at noon. He helped the students with the plants and seeds for their gardens, each student having a garden plot forty by sixty feet at the school which he had to tend and from which he received full return.

A writer from a nearby city newspaper visiting the school asked about a music program for a one-room school with children of all ages. The teacher called in those students who were in the orchestra. The teacher played a fine old-fashioned pump organ, and two mandolins, two ukuleles, a guitar, and a violin made up the rest of the orchestra. Much to the amazement of the visitor, the one-room "little red schoolhouse" made very fine music with that strange combination of instruments. With the ground-breaking for the Bomber Plant, Willow Run's "little red schoolhouse" became a bit of history.

The original school in our district dates back to the time when Michigan was still a territory. It was a log structure, twenty by twenty-four feet, and was completed in 1834. A frame building replaced the original structure in 1849 at the great cost

Old Spencer School

Foster School

Ross School

Simmonds School

of three hundred and fifty dollars. This frame school building was named Spencer School for Burke Spencer who lived in the Mansion House on Michigan Avenue, which the federal government was later to use as headquarters for the administration of the "Willow Run War Housing Center." This school building, with many alterations and additions, served the district until 1932. From 1917 to 1926, the school was closed and the children all attended school in Ypsilanti.

Mr. Edward Simmonds, former member of the school board and one of our best known old-time residents, told us the reason. "By that time," he said, "the Normal College in Ypsilanti was becoming famous for its teacher-training program. They needed children so they could show the beginning teachers how to teach. They asked us to send all of our children to their school in Ypsilanti."

At that time there was an interurban streetcar line that ran all the way from Detroit to Jackson. "The fare from our stop into Ypsilanti was a jitney," said Mr. Simmonds (a "jitney" was five cents). "It was cheaper for the school board to pay the transportation for the children to go into Ypsilanti than it was to operate Spencer School."

Spencer School was reopened in 1926 because the Normal College could no longer accommodate all of the children in the district. The old frame schoolhouse, in spite of its many alterations and repairs, was worn out and old-fashioned, so it was replaced in 1932 with a modern two-room brick building which cost $15,000. This structure is now the front part of the present Spencer School.

For many years Michigan State Normal College used Spencer School as a training school for rural teachers. In 1931, sixty-one children attended the school. The school was enlarged in 1942 to accommodate the additional children who had moved into the area, the enrollment that year being 145 pupils. This addition to the building was made possible through a grant of money from the Public Works Administration, an agency of the United States government.

When we look at our school system today, with its many fine buildings, including a new high school under construction, we realize that great changes have taken place in a very short time.

In the summer of 1941, the Bomber Plant and the airport were being built. That

The Grave Marker in Spencer Schoolyard Commemorating Those Buried in the Former Cemetery

summer the school board approved the hiring of a full-time janitor for Spencer School. The job paid fifty dollars a month. Another problem that had to be considered that summer was the request submitted to the Public Works Administration for funds to build an addition to the school. This addition was to be located on land which was part of a cemetery.

In October of 1941, the school board voted for a plan to attempt to contact relatives of all the people who were buried in that cemetery and obtain permission to remove the old, sunken, weather-beaten grave markers. It took Mr. Simmonds and Mr. Foster, another board member, until the following July to get final clearance to change the cemetery. They were authorized to remove the old markers, to get the ground leveled, and to place a single grave marker on the corner of the property in commemoration of those buried there. That marker is the one which now stands toward the front of the Spencer schoolyard.

Mr. Simmonds told me how he accomplished part of the job: "I knew they were doing all the construction over at the Bomber Plant, and that meant moving around a lot of dirt. It occurred to me," said Mr. Simmonds with a telling smile, "that if I could just get to see Mr. Henry Ford himself, maybe he would let us have some of that dirt they were digging at the plant."

Mr. Simmonds then made many inquiries of people who knew something of Mr. Ford's schedule. He waited at a place where Mr. Ford was supposed to make a daily appearance. "I recognized Mr. Ford when he drove up. I just went up to him and introduced myself—told him about the dirt we needed to level off that old cemetery for our schoolyard.

"Mr. Ford turned to the man with him and said, 'Harry, you see to it that this is taken care of.' Well," Mr. Simmonds continued, very pleased with his solution of the problem, "sure enough, the next day several loads of dirt were hauled over and dumped on the old cemetery." When the men had finished dumping the dirt, Mr. Simmonds asked them if they weren't going to level it.

"Nothing doing," said one of the men. "Not unless Harry Bennett tells us to do it."

"Well, then," said Mr. Simmonds, "I got in touch with Mr. Bennett, and in no time at all some graders from the plant came over and leveled off the schoolyard."

December 7, 1941, is known around the world as Pearl Harbor Day. On that day, part of the fleet of the United States Navy was attacked. Our country was at war. When this happened, all the people became conscious of the necessity to defend their country and their communities.

Accordingly, in March, 1942, the school board approved that Mr. McFall, the teacher, who had been asked to act as air raid warden, be given an order to purchase two cow bells to be used as air raid alarms, and that same month they met again and approved the purchase of two lanterns, two shovels, one crowbar, and an axe as air raid equipment.

The school board finally came to realize that their problem was not attacks from enemy bombers necessitating the ringing of cow bells, but the fact that thousands of war workers from all over the country were moving into the Willow Run area to work at the Bomber Plant. Something had to be done to provide adequate schools for the many children who were bound to come with them.

While our local school board was pondering this problem, various agencies of the federal government were making it possible to obtain help in such emergency situations. Representatives of the Federal Works Agency and the Federal Public Housing Administration worked with the school board so that applications could be made for funds to build additional schools and to hire the necessary extra teachers. Since the land the government had purchased on which to build the project of temporary houses was in Superior Township as well as in Ypsilanti Township, a new school district was established on July 22, 1943. This new school district included that area of Superior Township which had been purchased by the government, as well as the old school district located in Ypsilanti Township. This district was known as Ypsilanti School District Fractional Number 1.

During the summer of 1943, while the various parts of the housing project were being built, three schools were being constructed. These schools were named Foster, Ross, and Simmonds, after persons who were early residents of the area and who had served on the school board.

By this time, our nice settled community of big family farms was gone. In its place, we had a huge Bomber Plant with a production line three-quarters of a mile long and an airport with six runways. These six runways had enough concrete to make a highway twenty feet wide and one hundred and fifteen miles long. A community of temporary houses was being built, shelter enough to take care of from 15,000 to 20,000 people. The old Willow Run community was gone, but a new community with a future of great possibilities was rising in its stead.

PLANNING AND BUILDING THE VILLAGE

3

Henry Ford and the Ford Motor Company owned a great many acres of land in Washtenaw County at Willow Run. Because Mr. Ford and his company had vast experience in large industrial development and in mass production methods, they were chosen by the United States government to build the largest bomber plant in the world, where the famous B-24 bombers would be produced. Additional farm land was purchased by the government next to the Ford-owned land at Willow Run in order to have enough land for the Bomber Plant and for the necessary airport next to the plant to which the bombers would have easy access.

On July 23, 1941, the graders took to the field to make the airfield. The bull-dozers and graders roared and snorted as they dug and pushed the earth to level the land for the many miles of concrete runway. On December 4, 1941, the last paving was laid for the runways.

While the graders were leveling, Hansel "Tex" Brown from Ypsilanti flew over the area. Mr. Brown is now the credit manager of the Smith Furniture Company in Ypsilanti. He used to fly a Piper-Cub from the McEnnan flying field on Stony Creek Road. He knew as he flew over the area that, some day not too far away, a huge airport would be completed on the fields below.

"Wouldn't it be great," he thought, "to be the first person to land a plane at this Willow Run Airport?" He circled the small plane and came downstairs to have a better look.

"That field was still pretty rough," he told me, "but I came in easy until the wheels touched the ground, then pulled the stick and got back upstairs. I knew it was not safe to stop the plane and try to get a fresh start on such a rough field."

If Tex Brown was not the first person to land at Willow Run Airport, at least he was the first person to bring in a plane and touch the ground!

Site of the Bomber Plant and Airport Before Construction

Finishing Construction of the Bomber Plant

The First B-24 "Educational Model"

Willow Run Airport

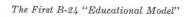

*The First PHA Staff at Willow Run—*SEATED: *H. V. Brontlinger, Clara Van Winkle, Sherwood Reeder, Guy Larcom, Stanley Pinel, Dorothy I. Cline, Emil Sheibel.* STANDING: *Morton Schaffren, Lawrence Green, William Gerhardt, Raymond Voight, Michael Martone, Lovey Newenhahn, Francis Servaites, Frank Kowalcheck, George Johnson, George Getz*

On April 18, 1941, the first ground was broken to start construction of the Bomber Plant. As soon as a section of the plant was completed, the manufacture of parts for the bombers was started. The first workers to be employed at the plant were Ford employees who were transferred from other Ford plants, but by the first of December, 1941, just seven days before Pearl Harbor, the plant had begun to hire outside workers.

The plant was designed to have space to do all the manufacturing of the B-24 bomber, the production of parts as well as the final assembly of the plane; the assembly line was to be three-quarters of a mile long. The plant was designed to employ from 50,000 to 100,000 workers, this number exceeding by five to ten times the number of people living in the city of Ypsilanti at that time, which was the city nearest to the plant—three and a half miles west of it.

In March, 1942, four months after the Bomber Plant began to hire outside workers, the Federal Public Housing Administration opened an office in Detroit. Mr. Sherwood Reeder was appointed as the director, and his office had the responsibility of getting housing built in those areas near Detroit into which the workers were coming. The most critical area was Willow Run.

There were not a great number of people living within a few miles of the new plant who were looking for jobs. Many of the workers came to Willow Run from farms and from little towns and crossroads. They came to Willow Run from Maine and from California—from all of the forty-eight states in the Union, and from Canada, Hawaii, and Puerto Rico. A few migrated from as far as our neighboring Latin-American countries.

People came to Willow Run on trains, on buses, driving their own cars. They came to get jobs. Although some people came merely to make money, others came because they wanted to contribute their efforts to help win the war. Some came for adventure. Workers by the thousand continued to make their way to Willow Run.

What happened to these people when they reached Willow Run? Where did they live? There were certainly not enough vacant houses, apartments, or rooms to rent to provide shelter for all this new population. What did these people do? Some of them slept in their cars. Some of them bought trailers and some pitched tents. Some built little shacks with scraps of wood and tin which they bought or scrounged. A few workers did find rooms and apartments in Ypsilanti. There was such a demand for housing that some landlords rented the same room to two different people: One tenant slept in the daytime and worked on the night shift, the other slept at night and worked on the day shift.

Some workers at the Bomber Plant lived in Detroit. Others lived in towns and cities even farther away than Detroit, some at a distance of sixty or seventy miles. Many of these people drove to the plant every day, a very tiring trip. Also, so much driving used up a great deal of gasoline and the rubber on tires, and by this time both tires and gasoline were rationed.

Because of the crying need for shelter, the Federal Public Housing Administration went to work. Construction engineers, surveyors, site planners, architects, all worked hard. They worked long hours, often far into the night, to develop a town near the Bomber Plant. Some place was needed which would provide housing for the thousands of people who were already in the area and for the thousands more who were bound to come.

"No, this plan won't do," said some of the people who had lived in Washtenaw County for many years. "You can never get enough water supply. What about sewage disposal?"

"It is not fair to use scarce materials to build houses when all materials are needed for guns, tanks, and planes to win the war," said others.

"Wait a minute," said a few. "It takes **people** to make the materials into guns, to build the tanks and planes to win the war. When you get the people to do this work you must have houses for them to live in."

Despite the fact that the United States of America was at war, our country called upon its tradition as a democracy, so that each group of citizens, whether they worked for a government agency or were local citizens of the community, had its chance to protest or to agree. There were many protests and arguments; citizens committees were formed. Finally, an investigating committee of the United States Senate was formed to look into the matter. The chairman of that committee was Senator Harry S. Truman.

After several months of considering and arguing the value of various plans, a compromise was reached. It was agreed that the Federal Public Housing Administration would build temporary housing, dormitories for single people and dwellings for family groups. This housing could be built on the land north of Michigan Avenue and south of Geddes Road, with the eastern boundary Ridge Road and the western, Prospect Road to Clark to Harris Road. This site was made up of ninety parcels of land with a total of 2,641 acres.

Late in 1942 the first contracts were let to build the dormitories at Willow Run. The surveyors came first with their rods and transits. Then came the men with the bulldozers, and next the men with the graders and trench diggers. When the surveyors finished a section, the diggers and graders went into action, scraping, digging, leveling.

There was no established water supply. The State Geology Department had been able to locate underground water for the Bomber Plant from their topographical maps which showed the early shores of the Great Lakes as well as of the Huron

Beginning Construction of Housing at Willow Run, Photographs Taken October 2, 1942

Just Eighteen Days Later, October 20, 1942, Construction Proceeds Rapidly

South Community and Administration Building

River. From this information, the drillers were also able to locate underground water for the Village. They built deep wells and pumping stations, well houses, and high storage tanks for the water. A sewage disposal plant was built. Water lines were laid, block by block, street after street, and sewer lines were laid to lead into the sewage disposal plant. Mile after mile of water line—mile after mile of sewage line. Finally, a total of thirty miles of lines were laid along the thirty miles of roads and streets in Willow Run Village.

When it rained, the mud was deep and sticky. The building workers got tired and grumbled. When it was hot and dry, the rough wind blew and tossed the sandy top soil which burned their eyes and stung their faces. The building workers got tired and they grumbled at the mud and at the hot dry dust. They grumbled but they kept going. They knew they had to get the job done for the thousands of people at the Bomber Plant who had no place to live. On and on they pushed. The people who built the weapons to win the war had to have shelter.

In February, 1943, the first dormitory was opened. It was in the dormitory project called Willow Lodge, which consisted of fifteen buildings containing 1,900

Willow Lodge Management Office and Post Office

rooms—some single and some double—with a capacity for 3,000 people.

In 1943 the Cleveland Regional Office of the FPHA sent Clara Van Winkle, now in the Management Office at Willow Run Village, to Willow Run as a Personnel Officer to help recruit people to work at the dormitories. They needed maids to clean the rooms, janitors to sweep the floors, and clerks to keep the records. Clara worked closely with Morton Schaffren, Assistant Manager at Willow Lodge.

"That was a really difficult job," Clara told me. "The Bomber Plant was hiring people with no training or skills and then sending them to a training school in the plant. The hourly rates of pay at the Bomber Plant for unskilled help were higher than the government paid. We listed our openings with the Michigan State Employment Office in Ypsilanti. We advertised in the newspapers. We did everything we could think of to get the people that were needed to do the work at the dormitories when they were opened."

"Did you make it?" I asked.

Clara laughed at that question. "I remember one morning sitting on the steps of the Mansion House with Mort Schaffren. Our office was in the Mansion House. This

38

a

b

c

Willow Court Trailer Project
Expansible Portable Community Unit
Holmes Road, with Family Trailers in Foreground,
Dormitories to the Left

was the day that our potential help was supposed to arrive. I suggested that if anyone did appear and if he or she had a pulse and could sign a name, that we hire them."

"What did Mort Schaffren think of your suggestion?" I asked.

"He said it was the perfect solution," Clara answered.

"How did you make out with your pulses and signatures?" I asked.

"We made out all right," she told me. "There were quite a few people who could not adjust to the hum and roar of the Bomber Plant who could do a good job of room cleaning and floor sweeping. We hired them."

The fastest way to get shelter for couples was to bring in trailers. By March of 1943, the first trailers in Willow Court were ready for occupancy. Within a few months there were 960 of these trailers. They were located north of Holmes Road and south of Clark Road, across from Foster School and behind Vercruysse's Grocery Store.

Francis X. Servaites, who is now director of public housing in Puerto Rico, was the first manager for these trailers. He wrote me about some of his early problems.

" I had managed a trailer project at Newton Falls, Ohio. I knew about some of the problems. The first thing I did was to get two pairs of field boots and I lived in them for months. These trailers had gasoline stoves. There was an overflow pipe that went through the floor of the trailer and deposited the gas onto the ground away from the fire. At the factory each of these overflow pipes had been carefully covered over by the floor insulation. When the first trailers were turned over to me I refused to accept them because of this fire hazard. The manufacturer was a bit put out with me but he fixed them up nonetheless. From then on it was street after street of inspection—dull plodding work. When we were in shape to go, we moved quickly with the renting."

The trench diggers and bulldozers continued to dig and grade. As soon as a street was laid, with the water and sewer line in, the big flat trucks rolled in carrying the prefab houses in sections.

a

b

c

Edward Eaton who lives on North Lamay Street tells us what it was like:

"First, a crew came along with hole diggers. They put in the posts for the foundations. Then came the crew that measured and leveled. They sawed off the posts that were too high, so the floors would be level. Then came the big flat trucks with the houses. That was really something to see. I could hardly believe my eyes. They had the flat trucks loaded so that the floor of a house was on the top of the load. A big crane lifted the floor down to the foundation posts. Then the carpenter crew nailed the floors to the foundation. Next on the load were the uprights and walls. Another crew put these up while the first crew had moved on to the next building. At the bottom of the truck load were the roof sections. They went on last."

The big trucks rolled in and rolled out. The cranes hoisted and lifted. The carpenters made things fit and nailed them together. As soon as a building was up, along came the plumbers and the electricians. The plumbers hooked up the outside water line, then connected the water faucets, sinks, and toilets. The electricians ran the electric wires from the fuse box on each building into the apartments, put in the wall plugs, and screwed down the fixtures.

On and on they moved, down street after street. Trucks, carpenters, plumbers, and electricians worked until there were temporary buildings that would provide homes for 2,500 families. Some of these houses were ready for tenants in June, 1943, and the project was finished later that year. This "flat-top" part of Willow Run was always called "the Village." These flat-tops contained four, six, or eight apartments with one, two, or three bedrooms.

The buildings with the peaked roof tops were in a section known as West Court and were built for couples or for three adults. Of the 1,000 apartments in West Court, some had no bedrooms and were called "zero-bedroom" apartments, and the rest had one bedroom. The first of these apartments was ready for occupancy in August, 1943. Another large dormitory project, containing 1,960 rooms and known as West Lodge, was also ready for tenants in August, 1943.

By the end of 1943 there were six different temporary projects in Willow Run: two of these were dormitory projects; one was a trailer project; another was a site for privately owned trailers with community laundry, shower, and toilet facilities;

Construction of West Court Family Dwellings

West Lodge, a Typical Dormitory

West Lodge Community Building

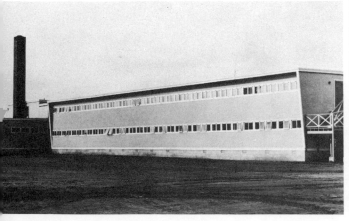

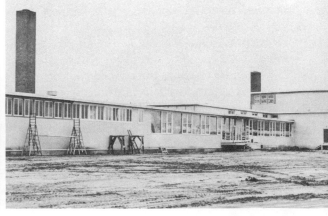

Village Commercial Area

two of the projects, West Court and the Village, were apartments for couples or families. All in all, there was shelter for more than 15,000 people, as many or more people than lived in the nearby city of Ypsilanti.

The government planners realized that if you are going to have rooms and apartments for thousands of people, you must have places for them to do their shopping, get a haircut, mail a letter back home, go to a movie, or have a place for some sort of recreation; so two commercial areas were planned and built. The south commercial area is where the Kroger store, the Willow Run Department Store, and the automatic laundry are now located. The north commercial area is where we now have the A & P grocery store, the barber shops, Cunningham's Drug Store, the shoe repair shop, Justice of the Peace Cowling's office, the dentist's office, and the Willow Run Post Office. A department store was built and operated by the Federal Department Stores in the space behind the A & P grocery toward the cab stand, but this building was destroyed by fire on Thanksgiving Day, 1944.

North Community Building Auditorium

Willow Lodge Cafeteria, North Community Building

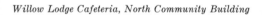

Willow Lodge Dormitory and Administration Building

Canteen in Willow Lodge Community Building

Fireplace in Willow Lodge Community Building

Typical Dormitory Lounge, Willow Lodge

The government planners also realized that if you are going to have a community of thousands of people, it must have a fire department and a police department. They planned and constructed the building which houses the Washtenaw County Sheriff's branch office and the Willow Run Fire Department on Stamford Road. To meet the people's need for entertainment, a movie theatre with a seating capacity of 1,200 was built, the Center Theatre near the Sheriff's office.

The Willow Lodge Dormitory Project had a community building with a cafeteria and a small theatre which showed newsreels. This building was torn down when the dormitory buildings were removed.

West Lodge Dormitory Project had a community building containing a large gymnasium and cafeteria. When the need for the dormitories had passed, so that no need for the West Lodge Community Building existed, our school board purchased it from the government and had it repaired and remodeled. Some of our boys and girls in the fourth, fifth, and sixth grades now attend classes there. The pupils in the Willow Run schools had a "school-naming" contest, and they chose the name of Holmes School for the newly acquired building.

The Teen Canteen on Clark Road was built as a community building for the trailer camp, Willow Court. When the trailers were moved away, this building became known as Spencer Annex. There was not room enough in Spencer School for all the children in that part of the school district, so this building served as an addition to it.

The North Community Building was erected next to Simmonds School. This is the building which now houses our library and in which the boys and girls at Simmonds School have their gym classes. Evenings and week-ends there are boxing teams, basketball games, and community programs here.

The South Community Building is behind the Kroger store, next to the bowling alley. After the war, when University of Michigan students came to Willow Run to live, this building was called the University Community Center. The building was operated by the University of Michigan.

While all of this construction of houses was going on, another unit of government, the Federal Works Agency, was building new schools. The Congress of the

United States approved funds for this agency to use in building schools in those communities where there were new war plants.

Building, building, building at Willow Run. In addition to the houses, the stores, the community buildings, and the schools, the building of the Bomber Plant continued. The Bomber Plant, which had had the head start in building in early 1941, was completed early in 1942; the airfield next to it was started on July 23, 1941, and completed in four months. To encourage workers to come from Detroit and surrounding areas to the Bomber Plant, a double super-highway, the Expressway, was built. It was completed and dedicated near the plant on September 12, 1942, by Judge Robert Patterson, who was then Undersecretary of War.

When it was decided that the Ford Bomber Plant was to be built near Willow Run, the land adjacent to the Ford land was purchased. Part of this land was Walter Wiard's farm and orchard. Wiard is a familiar name, since it is the name of the main road running north and south at the eastern end of the housing project.

Mr. Wiard wanted America to win the war, and he wanted to do what he could to help, but after he had sold his land, and when he saw what happened to it, he couldn't help feeling sad: "It took me twenty-nine years to plant, cultivate, and make that a fine orchard. It took those tractors and bulldozers just twenty-nine minutes to tear it down."

Building, building, building all over the United States of America during the first years of the war. Plants were necessary to build materials into guns and tanks and planes, to build the ammunition to win the war. Highways were essential to get the people to the plants so they could produce the materials to win the war. Temporary houses came into being to shelter the people who worked in the plants to help our soldiers win the war.

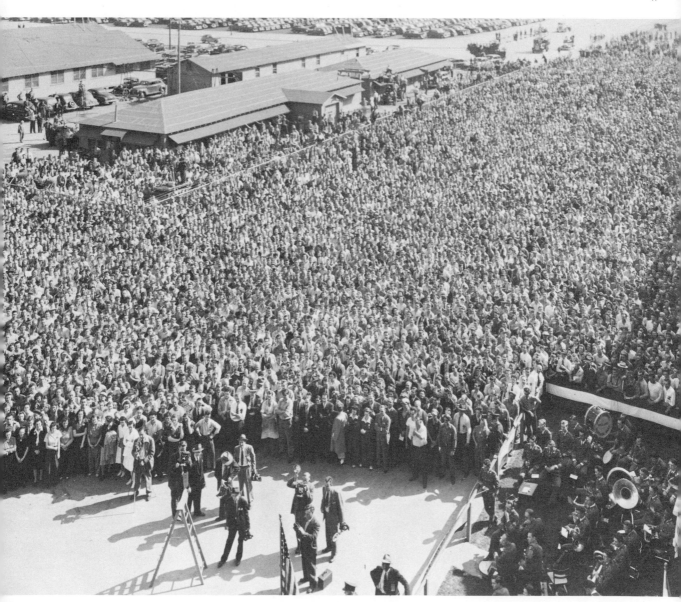

a

b

c

THE PEOPLE–1943 TO 1945

*Scene at Willow Run, Cafeteria Entrance
The Shuttle Bus Going to and from the Plant
In Willow Lodge Cafeteria*

It was the spring of 1943. A visitor had come to see the temporary housing at Willow Run. "This place looks and acts like stories of the Alaska Gold Rush," he said, "everybody is in such a hurry."

The visitor watched the big trailer buses called "cattle cars" roll up in front of the office. Workers scrambled off the bus, then hurried to the line at the post office. Names were called and letters from home eagerly snatched. As soon as the workers got their mail, they hurried off toward the cafeteria or to a dormitory building. Hurry, hurry, hurry. As soon as a bus was unloaded, another group of workers who had been standing in line, lunch buckets in hand, climbed aboard. The bus rolled back toward the plants and another pulled in. There were a great number of women in the groups of workers, many wearing slacks and work caps with visors.

"This is unbelievable," said the visitor. "This section of Michigan was just a nice area of good farm country. Look at it now. A regular little boom town. Just look at all the business here. There is the cafeteria, the barber shop, the post office—even a beauty shop. And so much building going on. There must be thousands of bomber workers here."

The first dormitory was ready for occupancy in February, 1943. From then until August of that same year, more and more buildings were going up, and as they were ready, more and more people moved into them.

It was in June, 1943, that the Bomber Plant reached its peak of employment, more than 42,000 workers. By January, 1944, when there were nearly 14,000 people living in the temporary houses, there were 35,644 workers at the plant. This shows that many of the people who worked at the Bomber Plant did not live at Willow Run, but were driving to the plant from their homes in Detroit, Wayne, and other towns nearby.

lie Schultz Working on a B-24

Mr. and Mrs. Ferdie Schultz are true Willow Run pioneers. For the first seventeen months they worked at the Bomber Plant, each of them drove back and forth to the plant from their home in Holly, Michigan. They now live on Quincy Court in the Village.

"I worked on one shift and Ferdie worked on the other," Margaret Schultz told me. "For weeks at a time we saw each other just long enough to say hello or goodbye." The distance to Holly is forty-nine miles. Mrs. Schultz said that when she was on the day shift the group with whom she drove left at five o'clock in the morning. They did not get back home until after six in the evening. "We certainly were glad when those trailers were ready," she said. "At least we did not have that long tiresome drive every day."

In order to understand what it was like at Willow Run during the war years, let us talk to some of the Willow Run pioneers who came here to work and live.

Marcia Potter is a doctor. She now lives in Ypsilanti and has an office there. When anyone asks Doctor Potter when she came to Ypsilanti, her answer is, "I came with the bombers."

Because of the war there was a shortage of doctors. Many of them were in the armed forces. Young men who ordinarily would have been studying for the medical profession were serving their country. The doctors who were left to take care of the people at home were the older men and the woman doctors.

Dr. Estelle Ford Warner was another of these women. She worked for the United States Public Health Service, and since, during the war, the doctors, engineers, and nurses with the Public Health Service were commissioned officers in the United States Army, Dr. Warner was a Lieutenant Colonel. She was assigned by her superior officer to attempt to find doctors to care for communities which were new, which were coming into being because of war plants. Her territory included Willow Run, Michigan.

Dr. Potter had started a good practice in Northville, Michigan. She had not thought much about Willow Run because she was too busy taking care of the people in the town in which she lived. Dr. Warner came to see her.

"Why don't you come to Willow Run?" said Dr. Warner. "People are coming from all over the country to work at the Bomber Plant, and they need doctors badly."

Dr. Potter thought about it. "Why should I move there? I have a good practice right here. I'm needed here."

Dr. Warner said, "Think about going to Willow Run. Willow Run is a place for people with courage—for doctors with courage, who are willing to be pioneers." She paused for a moment, then reassured Dr. Potter: "Don't worry about being needed, about being busy. You will be too busy at Willow Run."

Dr. Potter decided to be a pioneer doctor. Her first office was in the apartment at 1214 Rutland Court, as there were no office buildings ready at that time.

"The first thing I remember about that office on Rutland Court," said Dr. Potter, "was the terrible cook stove. I wondered how on earth we could ever get hot water." A great many people who had been accustomed to better facilities before they came to Willow Run, pondered the same thing.

"I had a woman working for me," continued Dr. Potter, "who came from a farm in the Upper Peninsula. She took one look at that stove, then got busy and built a fire. The woman said the stove was a wonderful stove. She said she would give anything to be able to buy one and take it back to her home in northern Michigan. I did not fuss about the stove any more. My helper loved it and made it work, and we always had all the hot water we needed."

Robert Stevenson, our Assistant Superintendent of Schools, is another Willow Run pioneer. Dr. Malcolm Rogers was hired by our school board as the Superintendent of Schools in the summer of 1943, and he hired Mr. Stevenson to come to Willow Run to be a teacher and, later, a school principal. Mr. Stevenson moved into a Willow Run Village apartment on Armistice Day of 1943.

"I wanted to get my family settled," said Mr. Stevenson, "so I went into Ypsilanti to order some coal. I was not too sure about operating those coal stoves, but it was cold that day, and I was sure I could figure it out."

Mr. Stevenson scratched his chin as he went on. "You know, I guess I was not remembering that there was a shortage of everything in those war days. I went to a coal company to order some coal and they laughed at me. They told me that

they had more orders from their regular customers than they could take care of that day. They said that if I really needed some coal, they would lend me a bag and I could go out in the coal yard and shovel some coal into the bag. They thought they might be able to get a delivery out to my apartment in the Village in a few days. Well, I went out in that coal yard and dug and scratched in that coal pile until I got enough to fill the bag. I took it back to my apartment and finally got a fire started."

Mr. Stevenson, Dr. Potter, and many others of our Willow Run pioneers were never too happy about those coal stoves. Of course, coal stoves were put in the apartments because this community was too far away from an established community to get gas. There was a serious shortage of oil because of the war, so it was not practical for the government to install oil heaters and cook stoves in the apartments. The only answer for a big little town out in the country was to provide stoves that would burn coal or wood. As Dr. Potter's helper thought, the cook stoves were good stoves. But, it happened that some of the government planners did not know enough about such stoves, which brings up what is, in retrospect, quite an amusing story.

It was a late November day in 1943. The day was hazy. The coal smoke hung heavy on the flat roof tops. Mr. Stevenson, who was then a teacher at Foster School, walked down Richmond Court toward Springfield. He noticed a funny-looking brown rock on the sidewalk which he kicked. It did not feel like a rock. He looked ahead and saw a great many little brown rocks in the yards and on the walk. Then he discovered the reason. A kitchen door flew open, and a disgusted housewife tossed a pan of little burned biscuits out toward the street.

"When they installed the stoves," Mr. Stevenson explained, "four-inch pipes were put in from the stoves to the chimneys. The pipes were not large enough to give the stoves sufficient draft. On a hazy day it was miserable. The ovens stayed cold, or suddenly became hot. The apartment grew smoky. On many hazy mornings, I kicked little burned biscuits all the way to Foster School."

The people who lived at Willow Run complained bitterly about the stoves, so the Management Office hired some engineers to investigate the problem. They learned that the people who were complaining had a right to be annoyed. To correct the problem of the stoves, the Detroit Field Office of the Housing Agency approved a "change order" so that all of the four-inch stove pipes were taken out and six-inch pipes were installed. After that, the stoves worked much better. The breakfast biscuits did not get burned and tossed out of the kitchen door on hazy mornings.

The cook stoves were just one of the many problems which made living in Willow Run difficult. Instead of electric refrigerators with which most families now are blessed, each apartment had an icebox. When you have an icebox it means that in order to keep your food from spoiling, you must arrange to have ice delivered. In hot weather, ice was needed every day, in cold weather, every second or third day. It also means that the drip pan under the icebox which catches the water from the melting ice must be emptied regularly. Getting ice and emptying drip pans created many problems for the Willow Run families.

Mrs. Marcella Church and her husband Parks lived in a trailer in Willow Court. Mrs. Church told us about the problem of getting ice. "With both of us working, getting ice for that little trailer icebox was really a problem. We never knew what time of day the iceman would come. We finally had to take a chance and leave our door unlocked with the ice money on the table so the iceman could get in. He was a most co-operative iceman and he would leave the ice, get his money, and snap the latch on the door as he went out."

Some residents figured out a way to stop the worry of the drip pan. They bored a hole in the kitchen floor, inserting a funnel in the hole. The hole and funnel had to be located directly under the drip hole to the icebox. The Management Office did not approve of this method of getting rid of melting ice, since there was the chance that floors would be rotted and that the drip water would encourage cockroaches to come up under the houses. Whenever an inspector from the Management Office discovered a kitchen floor with a hole in it for the icebox drip, he ordered it plugged.

The stoves smoked. The iceboxes dripped. The people had yet another problem. They had trouble finding where they lived. The trailers all looked alike and the dwellings all looked alike.

Margaret Schultz told me a story about one time when she became quite annoyed at her husband Ferdie. The Schultz's lived in a trailer in Willow Court on M Street. It was a lovely Saturday afternoon in the spring and they had made plans to drive back to their home in Holly, Michigan. Mr. Schultz wanted to get cigars at the drug store before they left, so his wife suggested that he make his purchase while she tidied up the trailer.

"Don't take too long," she suggested, "we want to get on our way as soon as possible."

The trailer was cleaned, her week-end bag packed, then she sat down and waited. Her usually prompt husband did not appear. She waited and fumed. It was not like Ferdie to take that much time to go to the drug store when they were so anxious to get away.

"An hour later," Mrs. Schultz said, "I looked out and saw Ferdie coming up the street. He had a sheepish grin on his face. 'What's the matter with you?' I asked crossly, 'I suppose you are going to tell me you got lost!' "

He shrugged his shoulders, laughed a little, and told her, "I did get lost. While I was over at the drug store they changed the name of the street from M Street to Melrose. I had to go over to the office to find out what happened to M Street."

A story is told about a lady who lived on Sudbury Court. On the day she moved in she looked for something to serve as a landmark so that she could remember in which house she lived.

"I noticed that the end apartment, next to Berkshire, had a bed spring leaning against the building and I decided that if I looked for the bed spring, I would know where I lived."

This signpost was very helpful to her for several weeks. In fact, it was so helpful that she never learned her house number. One afternoon after work she started for home. Suddenly she realized that she was lost; she could not find the bed spring! Someone had taken it away. After that experience, she remembered the house number of her apartment.

How to keep clothes clean was another problem shared by all the Willow Run people. Commercial laundry service was slow and undependable. The laundries had trouble getting the necessary help since most people who worked preferred to work in a war plant. The trailer project known as Willow Court boasted a laundry house in which there were electric washing machines. For a dime deposited in a meter, a machine ran for fifteen minutes. Many people stood in line for hours waiting their turn to get their washing done.

But before food can be cooked or preserved, before clothes can be washed, food and clothing must be available. Mrs. Nell Barrett, head librarian at Willow Run, and her husband Albert lived in the Village. Mrs. Barrett once told me, "I'll never forget that first few days. Albert went over to a store and managed to get some orange crates to use for wood to build a fire in the stove. I picked out the three best crates and saved them for extra cupboards and bookcases. We had a solitary cooking pan. I remember after the fire was coaxed into being, I heated the beans in that pan. After we ate the beans, I washed the pan so we could use it to make coffee."

During those war years, many basic items of food were rationed. Each family had to go to a ration board and apply for a ration book in order to buy meat, butter, sugar, or certain other supplies. In addition to the rationing of food, there was rationing of gasoline, tires, and shoes. Even unrationed items were frequently difficult to get. It was not unusual for one neighbor to tell another, "Better hurry over to that little store on the corner. A shipment of soap flakes just arrived."

The people of Willow Run had many problems and hardships, but they shared these problems and met them bravely. They realized that their living here was only temporary. They had come to work at the Bomber Plant. Some wanted to make money, others to help with the war effort, but they all looked forward to the end of the war so that they could return to the stability of the homes and communities they had left behind.

THE COMMUNITY–1943 TO 1945

rist Chapel (Sponsored by the Lutheran Church)

Dorothy I. Cline, Assistant Professor of Government at the University of New Mexico, worked for the FPHA at Willow Run as Area Director of Project Services. She worked with all of the local groups and agencies which provided community services for the residents of Willow Run, and she supervised those FPHA staff members who were assigned to special community activities. Her final written report, "The Willow Run War Housing Community—July, 1943, to July, 1944" gives us much factual information about those agencies and organizations.

The FPHA established the Willow Run Fire Department in May, 1943, to provide for the public safety. With the appointment of a trained Fire Chief, Frank R. Jacot, the state Fire Marshal, Arnold Renner, loaned a fire truck to the Village. The first fire station was located in a building, which has since been torn down, on the land south of the new Willow Run High School. The Fire Department was moved to the building on Midway, which is now the Willow Run Food Store, in March, 1944, and in October of that year, it moved to its present location on Stamford Road.

Miss Cline's report tells us that the FPHA made a contract to pay a specified sum of money to the Washtenaw County Sheriff's Department to provide police protection for the Village. This type of contractual service has been continued.

The Washtenaw County Health Department, under the leadership of Dr. Otto Engelke, County Health Director, set up a branch office at Willow Run, which has given service to the community since its establishment. The Well-Baby Clinic operated by this office has contributed a great deal to the health of our young people.

North Community Building, Willow Lodge

Infirmary

The United States Public Health Administration opened a forty-six-bed infirmary in July, 1943, located in the area between Willow Run High School and Michigan Avenue.

The first religious services were held in the auditorium of Willow Lodge, the community building which served the residents of the dormitories. These services were interdenominational. In December, 1944, the National Lutheran Council dedicated the Willow Run church known as Christ Chapel, which is located on Midway Boulevard and which, through all the following years, has held services for our residents.

The Archbishop of the Detroit Diocese appointed a chaplain to the Willow Run Mission in February, 1942. The Chaplain planned for the leasing of land from the federal government and for the construction of a chapel thereon. The blueprints for the church were completed in June, 1943. Eleven months elapsed before the chapel was opened for services, though, due to the problem of getting materials necessary for construction. The Mission developed a number of community organizations: the Holy Name Society, St. Vincent de Paul, Catholic Youth Organization, and St. Alexis Altar Society.

Local 50, UAW-CIO, was the union at the Bomber Plant. Local 50 was recognized as an independent local in 1943, holding its first election in July, 1944. Its Recreation and Education departments became interested in the development of programs in the war housing projects with the opening of Willow Lodge in February, 1943. Movies, dances, community sings, and special events were sponsored, and the organization of a tenants' association was begun. The Local also co-sponsored Halloween parties and organized a softball league. A paper called the **Bombardier** was published to keep the union members informed about the special activities.

The first American Legion Post, the Edsel B. Ford Post, 379, was organized at Willow Run in October, 1943. The Post purchased a log cabin and adjacent land on Michigan Avenue, opposite the Mansion House, which was its headquarters for several years. The Legion sponsored regular Saturday night dances at West Lodge and, at Christmas time, they gave a children's party.

A fine community service provided by Miss Cline's staff was the Information

The Mansion House

Office which had its quarters in the Mansion House. The work of the Information Office fell into the following categories: (1) to serve as a clearing house, (2) to disseminate information, and (3) to maintain reference materials and a photograph file. Below are some of the typical questions which were asked at the Office:

"Where can I get a driver's license?"

"Where is Public Works? I want to see if something can be done to lay the dust in the streets. You can't keep anything clean here."

"We want to get married **now.** Where do we go?"

"Where can I get permission to pick the cherries in the orchard? I want to can them for cherry pies this winter."

"How can I find my brother? He is supposed to live here somewhere."

"Can I buy one of these houses?"

In addition to answering questions, the Information Office organized tours for visitors who came to Willow Run. The Bomber Plant was national news, so, from the start, the war housing community of Willow Run shared this publicity. People from all parts of the United States, Canada, and South America having business in this part of Michigan came to see the Village. Among them were writers, research students, professional workers, and public officials. A variety of interests inspired the tours. Some were interested in the architecture of the temporary dwellings. Others wanted to see the community buildings, the infirmary, and the shopping centers, or to visit a typical dwelling unit or dormitory room.

Because of the lack of communication channels for the 13,000 residents in the community, three attempts were made at regular publication of Project newspapers during 1943–44. Although many persons were interested in publishing a newspaper, there was the problem of getting such a job done with volunteer labor, besides the problems of financing and distribution. None of the newspapers lasted longer than a few months.

The organization of resident groups such as the Resident Council and the Tenants' Association had similar problems. Many people were in favor of some organization to represent the residents but there were not too many who were willing to contribute time to it. There was also the problem of changing shifts at the Bomber Plant. A good resident committee would begin to function, then several of its key people would be changed to another shift, making regular meetings extremely difficult.

Perhaps the greatest factor making the organization of community activities for residents difficult was the attitude of a majority of the residents that their living at Willow Run was temporary. This was not home—just a place to live while they worked long and hard hours. Their roots were elsewhere. They looked forward to the day when the war would be over and they could all go "back home."

THE VILLAGE BECOMES A GHOST TOWN

Many months before "Victory in Europe Day," the thousands of workers at the Bomber Plant had achieved a great record. They were producing a complete bomber, the B-24 Liberator, every hour of every day, a production record that was praised whenever Willow Run was mentioned. As the efficiency at the plant increased, fewer workers were needed, so that by early spring of 1945, the total labor force was down to 16,000 workers. Gradually, people had begun to leave Willow Run to return to their home communities. After V-E Day the plant stopped production and planned only to finish the planes that were already under construction. Although the war in the Pacific area was still being fought, there were enough bombers in Europe that could be transferred to that area. After the plant stopped production, hundreds of people left Willow Run every day. During June, 1945, more than one thousand families moved out of Willow Run Village.

Alma Hensley, who worked in the Rental Office at that time and who presently does the same kind of work for the Village, told me, "We were really swamped. People came in by the dozens and tossed their keys on the counter. They did not bother to sign a Vacate Notice. They just told us they were going home."

Miss Hensley smiled and shook her head as she continued. "Some people didn't tell us they were leaving. When the next month's rent was due and not paid, we would go out to the apartment and find that the people had moved out."

Fay Christ is one of our pioneer teachers at Willow Run. She came here to work at the Bomber Plant, but after several months as a parts stamper, she decided to go back to her own field of teaching. Miss Christ accepted a position with the Willow Run schools and started work in September, 1943. She told us about the late spring of 1945. "There were forty-five children in my first-grade class at Foster School before V-E Day. At the end of the school term in June, only twenty-four children remained."

If Miss Christ's classroom was typical, it meant that nearly half of the children in our school system left to go home with their parents before the school year ended. "It was a continual caravan," Miss Christ said. "The people who owned their own trailers and who had lived in the trailer camp were the first to go. They just hitched the trailers to their cars and pulled away. I can still see that steady procession moving along Holmes Road."

Al Vercruysse, who operates the Willow Run Food Store, had had a store in an old building on Centennial Street. The building which his store now occupies at the corner of Clark and Midway used to be the Fire Department building. Mr. Vercruysse was born in Belgium, and in 1945 his mother and other relatives still lived there. As soon as the war in Europe had ended, he was anxious to visit his mother to make sure she was safe and comfortable.

"I left to visit my mother in October, 1945," Mr. Vercruysse said. "When I returned in February of the following year, my wife told me that the housing agency wanted us to move our store over to the Fire Station building. Many of our customers had been from the trailer camp. I could see why it was a good idea to move the store. All of the trailers were gone."

For the mutual protection of the people who remained, the Management Office made arrangements for them to move into apartments in the central part of the Village. That is why some of our families who are Village old-timers now live on Norfolk, Rutland, and Sudbury.

For greater efficiency and to reduce expenses, the Federal Public Housing Administration combined the several staff groups from the different projects and established a single management staff. This staff was housed in the office which has continued to be the Management Office, on Stamford Road next to Simmonds School.

As the months rolled by in 1945, more and more families left Willow Run. In December of that year there remained less than 600 families. Street after street was lined with empty buildings. The Village was nearly deserted. Just two and one-half years before, a visitor had remarked that Willow Run seemed like a town from the days of the Alaska gold rush. Again the Village resembled such a town, but after the gold was gone, and, with it, the people who came to find the gold. The Village had become a ghost town.

Mr. and Mrs. Parks Church lived in the Village at that time. They decided to go back to their home in North Carolina for a Christmas visit.

"When we left for home on that bleak December day," she told us, "we were sure that we would just come back to Willow Run and pack up and leave for good. All of the trailers had been moved out, the dormitories were closed, and they were talking about tearing down the buildings."

Marcella and Parks Church returned to Willow Run shortly after the first of January, 1946. They found a strange new wind whipping through the Village. There was rumor, talk, something the returning soldiers called "scuttlebutt." Something different was going to happen. Maybe the Village was not going out of business.

Strange new things did happen at Willow Run. The Churches did not pack up and go back to North Carolina, but continued to live and work in the Village. Now they are the proud owners of a new home on Harris Road below Holmes. Their architect and builder is another Village resident, Richard Wagner, who lives on Granby Court.

"I am certainly glad," said Mrs. Church, "that when we went home for that Christmas vacation we did not go permanently. Just look what we would have missed!"

HOUSING FOR HOMECOMING GI'S

7

The war in the Pacific area ended on August 14, 1945, the date that terminated a world-wide struggle.

Across America there were parades and celebrations. Factory whistles blasted. Automobile horns honked. Church bells rang. People laughed and cried, danced in the streets, and wept with joy. The chant echoed, "The war is over, the war is over."

"My son," said the mothers of soldiers, "When will he come home?"

"My brother," said their sisters, "When will he come home?"

"My husband," said the soldiers' wives, "When will he come home?"

There were small boys and girls who were anxious about the father they could not remember. "When will he come home, mother, when will he come home?" they said.

"When daddy comes home will we still live with grandma, mother?" asked some children.

"When daddy comes home," answered the war-weary wives, "we will get a place of our own."

"A place of our own," was the hope, the dream of the wives of soldiers who had stayed with relatives, and of sweethearts and soldiers who had been waiting to get married.

"A place of our own," was something the little children said and wondered about.

The end of the war found our men in service scattered all over the world. There were soldiers in Europe, in Africa, in Australia. There were sailors on ships on every ocean. Marines and Seabees were stationed on islands in the Pacific. Our men in fur-lined parkas were in Alaska and Greenland. They all prayed for that wonderful day when they would go home.

The leaders in our nation's capital worked frantically to move the boats, planes, trains, and buses bringing back the weary and homesick veterans. Day by day, week by week, and month by month, the thousands of men in the armed forces made their way back home to the country for which they had fought and to the families they had left behind, to continue their lives as peace-loving Americans.

The productive skill and energy of our people, as well as all available materials, had been used for the war effort to produce the guns, tanks, and planes to help end the war. The workers at the Willow Run Bomber Plant had produced a total of 8,685 B-24 Liberators. Of course, when the war ended, nothing had been done to build the homes that were needed for the returning soldiers and their families.

Willow Run Village had been built to provide temporary housing for war workers at the Bomber Plant, and everyone expected that as soon as the war was ended the Village would be torn down. The buildings were expected to last not longer than five years because they had been built with a minimum of materials only to meet the emergency.

What could be done to provide the necessary hundreds of thousands of homes that were needed for the war-weary veterans who were returning? Since the workers had vacated much of the "Temporary War Housing," the United States Congress, to alleviate the immediate emergency, passed legislation changing these to "Temporary Veterans Housing."

During the war years, eligibility to rent an apartment in the Village had depended on employment at the Bomber Plant. The Congressional change made apartments in the Village available to veterans only. Exceptions were made to provide housing for families of service workers who were needed in the Village, like school teachers, nurses, or employees of the Management Office.

Early in January, 1946, the veterans began coming to Willow Run to find homes. Many of them were from Detroit and the surrounding area and had returned to their old jobs, but could not find houses or apartments for themselves and their families. Many men planned to attend school at the University of Michigan in Ann Arbor, or at Michigan State Normal College at Ypsilanti, but housing in Ann Arbor and Ypsilanti was inadequate to accommodate all of these married veterans.

Before the war, not many married men went to a college or university; they waited until they had finished college before getting married. But these young veterans who had spent some of their best years in the armed services felt that there was no time to be lost. They wanted to do two things at once. They wanted to get married and start a family and they wanted to complete their education. Before the war, most housing in any college town was in dormitories or rooming houses. There were very few apartments, so that colleges and universities all over the country were faced with the same serious problem of helping the young veteran find a home for his family so he could complete his education.

To help solve this problem, the Federal Public Housing Administration worked out a plan with the colleges and universities to move many of the trailers and apartment buildings from the temporary war housing projects to the nearby campuses of colleges and universities which needed housing.

Originally, there had been 1,000 apartments in the West Court area of the Village. After 31 of the peaked-roof buildings were moved away, there were 572 apartments left in the 72 remaining buildings, none of the flat-top buildings having been removed. When the GI's started to come to the Village there were 3,068 apartments. Of the less than 600 families who had continued to live in the Village after the Bomber Plant closed, many were not veterans. The Housing Administration, however, ruled that they could remain, but all new families moving in had to be the families of veterans.

Willow Run Village is eight miles from the University of Michigan. There was not enough extra land on the campus at Ann Arbor to put up all the temporary units that were needed for the incoming young families, so the University of Michigan and the Public Housing Administration reached an agreement whereby 1,200 of the furnished apartments at Willow Run would be assigned to such students. Several surplus government buses were turned over to the University to provide transportation.

A veterans organization subsidized a bus line which ran regularly between the Village and Detroit for those residents who worked in Detroit. It was almost impossible to get an automobile, as the manufacture of all automobiles had been stopped immediately after Pearl Harbor Day. The factories had been converted for the production of war materials and did not change back until after the war had ended.

Workers from veterans organizations, from the colleges and universities, and from the Public Housing Administration did everything they could for the GI who had come home. The use of this temporary war housing did make it possible for the returned soldier and his family to have "a place of their own."

Congress passed another piece of legislation which helped the men who wanted to get an education, the "GI Bill," which provided that each veteran could draw an allotment of money each month to cover his basic expenses while he attended school. Without funds from the GI Bill, many of them would not have been able to attend college, and the inexpensive rent at the Village also helped make it possible for thousands of married veterans to go to the University.

Evelyn Sorensen and her husband Robert moved into a zero-bedroom apartment early in 1946. I asked Evelyn what it was like.

"We had gone to the office at the University to inquire about a place to live, since Bob was enrolling at the University. They told us about the Village. A big bus waited out in front of that office until it had a full load of people going to the Village. They drove us out there."

Mrs. Sorensen smiled as she remembered. "It was snowy that January day. When we got out to the Management Office, the lobby was packed with people like us. Someone told us there was a model apartment we could look at, down on Monson Court. We walked down there through the snow. I remember I had forgotten my galoshes and my feet were soaked. Many other people had walked through that apartment. It was wet and dingy. I was so happy to have Bob back from the war that the wet, dingy apartment looked wonderful to me. We waded through the snow back to the rental office and signed a lease."

Evelyn and Robert Sorensen lived in the Village until the spring of 1950. During that time, Evelyn obtained a job in the accounting section at the Management Office while Bob continued his education. He earned his master's degree in music and in

education. "That was really an experience," Bob told me, "writing a master's thesis on the kitchen table in an apartment with no bedroom."

Since his graduation from the University, Bob has become head of the music department for the school system in Wayne, Michigan. The Sorensens own their own home on Colonial Drive in Inkster.

The story of the Sorensens is typical of several thousand GI families. The men wanted to complete their education, and the wives wanted to help. They managed to keep house in a Village apartment and many of them obtained jobs to augment the family budget, since the GI bill provided only the bare subsistence.

Some men came to the Village because their families had been living here while they were in the service. One of these was Andrew Grenier, who is now a member of our school board. While he was overseas, his wife and children lived in a Village apartment on Richmond Court. The Grenier family now live in their own home on Ford Boulevard. When Andrew Grenier left his family to go overseas, his son Garry was less than a year old. When he returned on December 3, 1945, Garry was two and a half years old. The first evening that Andy sat down to have dinner with his family, his son Garry looked at him strangely. Garry had been too young to remember his father, yet he realized that this man seemed very important to his mother.

Garry, trying to be friendly, looked at his mother and said, "Give the man a piece of pie, Mama."

Our men who served America during the war are all heroes. The wives of these men who helped make a home for their returning husbands, who brought up children without the help of a father, who suffered the hardships of Village coal stoves, who managed on very lean budgets, are also very brave.

A great many unmarried veterans also wanted to continue their education. The University of Michigan did not have enough dormitory rooms to accommodate this great influx of students, and since the Public Housing Administration had vacant dormitory buildings at Willow Run, the West Lodge Dormitory Project which had been built for the war workers was reopened for these single students. All of the buildings were for single men students except one building, which was reserved

West Lodge and Dormitories Opened for Single Students

First Dummy Model of the Kaiser-Frazer C

for single women students who were attending the University under the GI bill. All of the women living in that dormitory had been in the WACs, the WAVES, or the WAAFs and had the same rights under the GI bill as did the men.

Early in 1946, the Kaiser-Frazer Corporation obtained the Bomber Plant from the government. The company began to hire workers to convert the plant for the manufacture of automobiles, then hired workers to make the cars. Many of these employees were veterans who came to Willow Run to rent an apartment.

BOMBER NO. 139 COMES HOME

"Say, Mister," said a stranger to a resident of Ypsilanti, "How do I get to Willow Run Village? I have a brother who lives there and I want to look him up."

"Well, now," answered the local citizen, "the Village is a little east of here, north of Michigan Avenue." He scratched his ear and thought. "Tell you what," he said pointing east, "you will come to an old B-24 sitting under an apple tree. Turn left down the next road."

The stranger thanked him and started on his way, wondering why a huge plane was sitting under an apple tree.

Many of us who lived or traveled in the Willow Run area during those postwar years wondered about the old bomber. Who put it there? Why? I decided to investigate and I found out that one evening, late in 1945, several members of the Edsel Ford Post of the American Legion were meeting informally in the headquarters in a log cabin on Michigan Avenue across from Spencer Lane. They had all served their country in the armed forces, and many members of the post had worked at the Bomber Plant. But the push and hustle of the Bomber Plant was gone. The Village was a ghost town. The area was empty, quiet. One member suggested that a memorial should be erected nearby to commemorate the bomber.

"Let's write to Washington," said one man, "and ask them to send us a dummy bomb. We could have it set up out here and everyone would know that this is the area that made the planes that dropped the bombs." The idea seemed fine to the other legionnaires. A letter was prepared and sent off to Washington requesting a dummy bomb. In due time, a polite reply was received advising the legion post that they did not have such a bomb available.

"Tell you what's the matter with those fellows in Washington," said one member the next time they met. "They can't think about little things like a dummy bomb. They just think about big things." He thought for a while. "Why don't we ask them for a plane, a bomber? Maybe they have a spare one around they don't want." The speaker was half-joking but thought the idea worth trying.

Several of the legionnaires scoffed at the idea. "Why would they even consider sending us a bomber," added one, "when they turned us down on a dummy bomb that wouldn't be any more than a sand bag?"

"It won't hurt to try," said the man who had made the original suggestion.

After considerable discussion, the members finally agreed to send a letter requesting a bomber. There was not a man in the group who actually believed that they would get one. But, much to their amazement, their letter was answered promptly. The War Department would give them a bomber as a memorial. It would be flown in to the Willow Run Airport on February 26, 1946, for delivery. An official committee was hurriedly organized to give the bomber a proper reception when it arrived. The committee waited anxiously at the airport. "Suddenly we saw her, a giant graceful bird circling in for her last landing," said Albert Barrett who waited with the committee. He had served with the 90th Bomber Group, 5th Air Force, at New Guinea in the South Pacific. He was well acquainted with B-24's. "It made a lump in my throat to remember what this plane, and her thousands of sister planes, had accomplished."

The plane, Number 139, landed and eased over to the reception committee. One could see that she was a battle-wise veteran. The flight crew disembarked and, after a welcoming speech, the members of the Edsel Ford Post accepted full custodial responsibility. She was then taxied over to the apron of the airfield to await plans for transfer to her new home.

One committee of the post worked on plans for a fitting dedication ceremony. Another committee planned ways and means to transfer this huge, inert bird from the airport over to a spot near the headquarters of the post. The committee working on plans for the dedication had its assignment completed, but the committee working on transportation of old Number 139 had not arrived at a satisfactory solution.

Moving Bomber No. 139 Over the Railroad Spur

" That ship, which looked like such a graceful bird up in the sky, suddenly began to look like a monster gremlin," said one of the members. He had served in the Air Corps and knew about little gremlins. "We just could not figure out how to move her without a great many problems."

The dedication ceremony, to which important guests had been invited, was scheduled for Sunday, May 26, 1946. The committee in charge of transportation had not agreed on any plan but they had to do something. On May 20, they collected three tractors, a caterpillar and two smaller ones. The committee members had great will and determination.

Albert Barrett had helped on the transportation committee. He told me about it. "We didn't get her out of the Kaiser-Frazer yard that first day. K-F had run a railroad spur through the yard which was higher by a few feet than the rest of the area. We had to construct a ramp to get her over the tracks." He laughed as he continued, "When we got her up on that ramp, the old girl almost tipped over, but she righted herself. Guess she had more poise than we did. We were nervous."

The Bomber Traveling Along Ford Boulevard

The next day they removed part of the main gate to the plant to get old 139 out on Ecorse Road. "Things seemed to go smoothly for a while," Mr. Barrett continued. "We had the caterpillar tractor hitched to her nose wheel and a small tractor hitched to each side wheel. We got into trouble when we reached Ford Boulevard. A wing clipped a tree and the tree had to be removed. Then the highway signs interfered. The highway department was standing by, so they removed temporarily all the highway signs. The next obstacle was a utility pole. The crew from Detroit Edison removed that to let us through. We finally made it over to the Baptist Church on Forrest Avenue on the second night."

"Why," I asked, "did you finally park her in that apple orchard on Michigan near Spencer? Someone told me that the orchard was government property and you did not have permisison to put her there."

"That's right," Mr. Barrett said. "We had to get that ship moved and set up in time for the dedication. The orchard was government property but it was just across Michigan Avenue from the post headquarters. There was no room near our build-

Old No. 139 Being Parked Under the Apple Tree

ing. We seemed unable to locate anyone in authority who could give us permission to put her there. We decided to take a chance."

The dedication ceremony was held as scheduled, with Mr. and Mrs. Henry Ford as the guests of honor. The Edsel Ford Post of the American Legion had, of course, been named in honor of their son who had died.

The people who attended the dedication were proud and happy that old 139 had come back home to the place where she had been built. She had come back to the place where she had made her maiden flight, home to Willow Run.

They were proud of her war record. She was a great heroine. She symbolized the work of the men and women who had built her. She symbolized the courage and

Mr. and Mrs. Henry Ford at Dedication of Bomber No. 139

bravery of the men who had flown her in combat. Old 139 was a heroine who had earned her tribute.

She settled down under the apple trees but she was not happy. She was a sky bird, not a land bird. She was bothered by many earthbound creatures who picked at her wings, jiggled her struts, pulled bits from her tail. The months wore on into years. Bit by bit the plane lost its skybird glamour. Old 139 became neglected. No more did the people talk about her daring flights, of the times she had knifed through the air at 300 miles an hour.

Finally, in 1950, workers for a scrap metal company carefully removed her remains. Old 139's spirit is now free to sail the skies.

WILLOW RUN,
A PEACETIME COMMUNITY

To better understand the way of living in the Village during those first peacetime years, I asked some of my friends who were residents to tell me about it.

Carolyn Leithauser and her husband Richard were a pioneer student family. They moved to Willow Run in the fall of 1945. Carolyn later became the Social Director for the University Community Center. She told us that, when signing the lease, she had said to Mrs. Gladys Hammett, "I hope you give us an inside apartment; I'll freeze in one of the end ones." Carolyn was not too unhappy when she obtained her apartment, even though it was an end apartment on Quincy Court.

"The first thing we did after moving in," Carolyn told me, "was to order a ton of soft coal. This coal was quick to ignite, quick to give out heat, and quick to cover the fresh ivory paint with soot. We used seven tons of coal that first year to heat and cook with those monster stoves. But we were warm, we kept it clean, and we had showers whenever we wanted them. It was not like what we had seen in Ann Arbor where the signs stated, 'Room—bath privileges'."

Carolyn, like the people who lived in the Village during the war years, had her troubles with the cook stove. "I tried to make pear jam one day," she said. "The fire was at a nice steady heat for the jam to simmer properly. I checked the fire and felt sure that there was no possible chance for it to get any hotter—the glowing coals were on the ebb side, I thought. Everything under control, I skipped off to the store, just seconds away from my door, to get some paraffin. Only a minute, I said to myself. I came back in a minute to find the top of the kettle on fire! I beat it out with a wet broom and then collapsed in a chair, wondering how anyone could leave such an unpredictable monster alone! All would have been well if the wind hadn't suddenly drawn the fire a little more. Some days the wind was no help at all. It would seem to sit on the chimney."

Carolyn told of her problems washing clothes. During the first months she washed by hand in the deep sink. When she discovered the wash houses with their electric washers, she and her husband bought two bicycles and pedaled the laundry to the wash house each week. Drying clothes was a problem, because if there was another fire on the court—and there usually was—the nice clean clothes on the line were very apt to become covered with soot.

Carolyn told me about an exciting night in the Village. "Once during a storm, the lights went out all over the Village. We didn't call the neighbors on the phone—we rapped on the wall! Who has a candle? Dick must study! He has an exam tomorrow."

The Leithauser's apartment on Quincy Court was on the side toward the bowling alley. "We more or less moved right into the activity of the bowling alley," Carolyn said. "It was about 800 feet away from us, so we were quite familiar with strikes and spares, knowing them by their tune. We were often lulled to sleep by that bowling alley." The Leithauser's first spring at Willow Run was in 1946. "The first thing we did was to plant something! We put in four slips of box elders. We paid the Village a visit in the summer of 1954 and the trees at 1780 Quincy Court were the slips we had planted!"

Robert Cooper and his wife Lynn lived in the Village during those crowded busy days in 1946 and 1947. Bob was a student at the University of Michigan, working for a degree in engineering. I asked Bob to tell about his impressions of the Village in those days.

"I think of coal smoke and the Army." he told us. "I was a Weather Observer in the Air Corps. We used to go up on top of the Weather Office to read instruments and note visibility. On those early morning observations, sometimes all we could see were rows and rows of barracks, slightly obscured by a pall of coal smoke. We have all seen the same thing many times on a wintry morning in the Village."

"Another link with the Army," Bob continued, "is the similarity of buildings, the crowded conditions, the long lines for the school buses which were still painted olive drab. The buses made that convoy-like trek into Ann Arbor every day. More than that, the 'everyone in the same boat' feeling that existed in service carried right over into the Village. Buddies in the Village could have been your buddies in the Army. All in all, this carry-over was a big help."

Bob Cooper was in a reminiscent mood as he continued, "I'm sure that Village life was much harder on the student wives. For most of them, I guess, there was no corresponding transition-piece—nothing to take the sting out of the new conditions. For the ordinary dogface, familiar with cramped quarters and no privacy, the existence of a partition, even if paper-thin, was an improvement. To the new student wife, it must have been a step toward living in a goldfish bowl. The student could take it. He was there by his own choice, doing what he wanted to do. In most cases, the wife was only there sweating it out to be with her husband."

After some experience in private industry as an aircraft engineer, Bob is now completing his work at the University of Michigan for a Ph.D. in engineering. In summing up his feeling about the Village, he said, "The back pages of almost every technical publication are filled with advertisements begging for trained personnel to fill important industrial jobs. The squawks would be even louder if a lot of good men had not had the Village to help them attend school to qualify for many of these jobs."

I talked to Bob Cooper's wife Lynn about her feelings concerning the Village. "Shortly after Bob and I were married," Lynn said, "we spent a weekend in the Village with a couple of his friends. They were packing to move out, so the apartment was more crowded than usual, but they were so cheerful and friendly about inviting us to stay, even though it was crowded. I guess they knew how important the price of a hotel room was to us." Lynn smiled as she continued, "I went back to Chapel Hill to finish work for my degree. Bob got a room in one of the Willow Run dorms. He made application for an apartment so that as soon as I had finished school, and if an apartment were available, I could join him."

Lynn then admitted that, as an adoring young wife whose greatest desire was to join her husband, she disillusioned him at one point. "Bob had been calling me every Saturday night. Each week he would tell me sadly that there was no apartment. He told me to hold on and hope—maybe next week. When he called that final

Saturday, just vibrant with enthusiasm, and told me that we had a zero-bedroom apartment, I cried. I must defend myself by saying that after the initial shock, I recovered rapidly. I will skip the first couple of weeks when I tried to get used to the stove, to the sound of someone clearing his throat next door, to the icebox that constantly plugged, and the feeling that I was never really alone."

"Decorating," said Lynn with vehemence, "that was a challenge. When we discovered that we could tint the paint the management issued it was like finding gold. One of our student neighbors found a bargain on a huge batch of odd lots of heavy linoleum. When he had matched up what he could use, he offered the balance for sale as cheaply as he had bought it himself. We grabbed. I remember with pride the brilliancy of inlaid kitchen floor and sinktop, which consumed many of our hours. Some of our books are still marred with linoleum paste because we used the books to weigh down the linoleum as it dried."

Lynn told me about that first year in the Village. "I built and painted furniture, made drapes, dyed unbleached muslin and made curtains, turned sod and planted a lawn and flowers. I traded new ways of cooking hamburger with the other wives on the court. I think that at one time I had collected twenty-three recipes for hamburger. Life on the GI subsistence was not easy for any of us. I think that those wives who worked sacrificed the creation of a first 'home.' It took a long time before I honestly understood my husband's deep feeling that I must not work. He felt that unless he could support me, we should not be married. My job, therefore, was to learn to live within our means—not just exist—but to live a good life, a full life."

I asked Lynn Cooper how she felt about her neighbors in those hectic days. "Our neighbors were wonderful. We didn't know all of them, but we somehow counted on them in case of emergency. It was almost impossible to get a private telephone in those days. Of course, even if they were available, very few of us could have afforded them. There were many convenient telephone pay stations on the project at that time. We always knew that if there should be an emergency necessitating a phone call and if we did not have a nickel to make the call, one of our neighbors would gladly provide that nickel."

"You know," said Lynn thoughtfully, "the whole secret of those glorious days was something actually quite rare in our world's society—kinship. Our problems were basically the same. Our ages and our goals were basically the same. No one could be selfish and survive. We needed each other. We needed encouragement and sympathy and help. Beyond this, we needed to belong. I think we were like a family, a good family. We did not try to pry, but we were also willing to lend an ear. There was co-operation. No one walked on a garden or newly seeded lawn, no matter how close he might come to missing the school bus. Everyone's problems were very much the same. Everyone looked for a solution for the other fellow as well as for himself."

"Do you remember," I asked "any special highlight of those early days in the Village?"

"Do I remember!" Lynn beamed as she told us, "It was a night in late summer. We had finished our decorating, furniture building, making of drapes and curtains. The place was attractive and comfortable. Bob had quit studying for the night. We were drinking coffee in the living room and eating our weekly extravagance, a homemade ice cream sundae. Bob sat there with a look on his face I had never seen before. It was relaxed, happy, even smug. 'What are you grinning at?' I asked. He just looked at me for a few moments, smiling. Then he said, 'We have a home'."

COMMUNITY ACTIVITIES
IN THE VILLAGE

10

Social Directors at the University Community Cent(
Anna Rankin Harris and Carolyn Leithau(

"It must be very dull and boring to live in the Village," said an outsider during a visit. "No place to go, nothing to do, I don't see how the people stand it."

The outsider did not know how much many of the Village people enjoyed living there. The residents say that there was a community spirit, a feeling of neighborliness, that they have not found elsewhere, and that actually there was usually not enough time to do all of the things they wanted to do.

Carolyn Leithauser served as the Assistant Social Director for the University Community Center under the first Social Director, Anna Rankin Harris. When Miss Harris left to become Assistant Dean of Women at the University of Pennsylvania, Mrs. Leithauser was appointed Director. I asked Carolyn to tell me about the organization of the center.

"The University of Michigan realized that a happy student was apt to be a good student," she said. "Through a veterans' co-ordinator the welfare of student wives in the Village began to be considered. If they were not happy, it reflected in the veteran student."

The first co-ordinator from the University was Colonel Walter B. Farris. He left for another position and was replaced by Richard Correll who served in this capacity for several years. The co-ordinator worked out an agreement about the use of the community building. It was made available, rent free, for community activities. The PHA, which owned the building, provided heat, light, and janitor service. It was the responsibility of the University to employ a social director and any additional staff necessary to organize and promote programs that would be of interest to the wives of students. As the programs developed, all wives in the Village were welcome, whether or not their husbands were students.

The building became known as the University Community Center. It was open daily from 10 A.M. to 10 P.M. except on Saturday and Sunday. Special meetings, parties, and programs could be scheduled by making arrangements in advance. On Sunday, interdenominational church services were held in one room under the leadership of Reverend J. Edgar Edwards, an active and prominent Village resident. He represented the local Protestant ministers.

When asked how she knew what sort of activities would interest the wives, Carolyn said, "As each new semester began, the rental office, which was most cooperative, allowed us to check all the cards of new families. If they were student families, or young families, we called on them. We invited each new resident wife to come to the center and get acquainted."

Carolyn then told me that one of the first groups to be organized was called the Wives' Club. At the first meeting of each new school semester, a special program was planned for the new wives.

A lending library was established with the assistance of the University Library. When a family moved out of the Village, books that they no longer wanted were donated to the Library. A special room was prepared with adequate lights, tables, and chairs, to serve as a place for study. Reference books from the University were provided, and a part-time librarian was on duty. Many of the men students, particularly those with small children at home, did much of their studying in this library.

The PHA obtained some sewing machines, which were made available at the University Community Center. Almost any day that one visited the center, the humming buzz of the sewing machines could be heard. "Those sewing machines," Carolyn said, "were not only used by the young wives who were trying to be good homemakers. I recall that several of the men also came over to use the machines."

A group of wives who were interested in ceramics initiated the organization of a ceramics club. This club is still popular at Willow Run and has regular exhibits in the cabinet in the lobby of the Management Office. To start the club, the University provided a kiln, and the PHA electricians installed the necessary additional wiring to make its use safe.

he Willow Run Co-operative Nursery

The Willow Run Co-operative Nursery, which entered its tenth year of operation in the fall of 1955, was organized by a group of student wives. It had an original capacity of three nursery groups, with thirty children in each group. The classes were held in the gymnasium of the University Community Center. The PHA had in storage certain items of nursery school play equipment, used during the war years for the day-care centers, which were installed at the center for use by the Co-operative Nursery. Included were dozens of tiny canvas cots, the exact size for little folks' naps.

Unique elements of the nursery include a transportation service to and from school for the youngsters. At the beginning, a University bus carried the children. Later, a station wagon and driver were hired; today's system calls for a car pool arrangement of travel.

The group boasts a family-type relationship, with many brothers and sisters following one another through the years. As many as three children in a family have attended different sessions.

Tuition at the school is perhaps the lowest in the state, averaging less than fifty cents daily, this minimum being possible because of the low overhead expenses. The tuition makes it possible to employ a trained nursery school teacher, and to provide funds for the youngsters' daily snack.

The first nursery school teacher was Donna Warren. Since then, the teachers who have served have been Frances Morley, Betty Crawford, Elizabeth Stone Rima, Helen Kraybill, Alice Edwards, Helen Rucker, and Grace Aaron. Another part of the program of the nursery school has been that mothers of the children take turns assisting at the school. This gives the mother opportunity to observe her child as a member of a group of children his own age.

As the student population of the Village declined, the nursery school enrollment went down. In 1951 there were two operating groups, eventually dropping to one group by 1954. To date, nearly 500 children have attended the nursery school.

Officials who started with the Willow Run Co-operative Nursery have gone on to state posts. Mrs. Holbrooke Seltzer was president of the Michigan Council of Co-operative Nursery Groups in 1954, and Mrs. Elizabeth Downer is the secretary of this state organization.

Ypsilanti High School Girls Drum and Bugle Corps Lead the Halloween Parade

The Halloween Parade

Another special activity initiated by the Wives' Club was an annual Spring Style Show. Arrangements were made with local merchants to have the wives model new spring outfits. Some merchants donated merchandise for door-prizes. The money made at the Wives' Club Spring Style Show was always given to a worthwhile community project. Several of our "tot lot" play areas were financed by these funds.

At the end of the spring semester in 1954, the University discontinued its sponsorship of the Community Center. The number of student families had gradually decreased from a peak of more than 1,300 families to less than 150. With the discontinuance of the program sponsorship by the University, the PHA representatives proposed that the schools provide part-time leadership to continue the existing activities, and the Willow Run School Board approved this proposal. However, shortly after the schools began sponsoring the programs, the Chicago Field Office of the PHA advised the local Management Office that the community center building would be needed by the PHA as a headquarters to service this area of Michigan for PHA projects that were being discontinued elsewhere.

With the loss of the building, the school board approved the transfer of the activities from the community center building to the North Community Building. The Ceramics Club and the Co-operative Nursery School now have their quarters there.

In the early fall of 1946, Alfred Brose, the first Director of Recreation and Adult Education employed by our local board of education, called a meeting of representatives from the schools, the churches, the Resident Council, the PHA, the County Sheriff's office, the PTA, and other interested groups. This committee planned the first annual Kids Halloween Party, which became an annual event at Willow Run. When Mr. Brose left, the Willow Run management staff took over the responsibility of promoting the Halloween party, and in 1950 transferred it to the Resident Council, which worked in co-operation with school principals and teachers. On October 31, all the boys and girls went home from school to dress in their Halloween costumes. They reported back to their respective schools and, at a specified time, started a parade. The parade was headed by the red fire truck and the sheriff's car

with its flashing red light and whining siren. One year, the Ypsilanti High School Girls Drum and Bugle Corps, famous for its complex marching formations, led the Willow Run Kids Halloween Parade. The boys and girls paraded from their schools to the corner of Clark and Midway, then up Midway and across Stamford to the Center Theatre, where a committee judged the costumes of dozens of witches, skeletons, tramps, spooks, and other Halloween characters who walked across the stage for those showing imagination and originality. Each year twenty of the boys and girls were winners of prizes donated by our local merchants. After the costume judging, the Center Theatre showed a movie program, the management giving the use of the theatre, a good movie, and an operator for the movie projector. When the show was over and the children came out of the theatre, waiting for them were the fire trucks and the firemen with the trucks filled with bags of treats for each boy and girl.

The Grasshopper Club was another unique Willow Run organization. It was promoted by the management staff in co-operation with the school principals and teachers. Every school child was eligible for membership, if his mother or father signed a letter stating that the child had helped his parents do a good job of "Spring Clean-Up" in his yard.

Each Grasshopper received a Grasshopper button and a membership card. Early in May of each year, the manager of the Center Theatre donated the use of the theatre for a special movie program for the Grasshoppers, and the school principals allowed the Grasshoppers to leave school early on that day to attend the movie. In addition, many of our Grasshoppers learned that it was fun to work together to make the community neat and attractive.

Harry Caswell became our Recreation Director in 1951. He obtained the co-operation of the school administration, the PHA, and the Ypsilanti and Superior Township Boards to make the Teen Canteen a reality. The building which houses it had been constructed in the early days of Willow Run to serve as a management-community building for the trailer camp. Of course, when all the trailers were gone, the PHA no longer needed the building. For several years it was used for extra classes from Spencer School. Now the building is used for our Teen Canteen, which,

Grasshoppers at Work

Party at the Teen Canteen

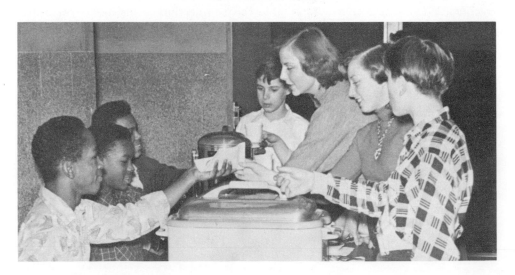

with its fine snack bar and club rooms, serves the young people of our community. There is a good gymnasium for dances, pool and ping-pong tables and equipment, and facilities for club meetings and parties. The area outside the Teen Canteen has been developed into an excellent community picnic area. There are outdoor fireplaces, and under the shade trees there is playground equipment for the young folks.

The summer playground programs are most popular with our young people. A special feature of these activities is the Story Hour, sponsored by the Willow Run Library. The library staff also arranged for special book collections to be loaned to the playground leaders so that readers clubs could be organized. Our local churches have always sponsored the summer Bible schools, which have been conducted each summer during the first two weeks following the end of the school semester. The daily summer programs include a bus to provide transportation to Portage Lake for swimming and camping. On several evenings during the summer, young people who like to roller skate are taken by bus to the nearby roller rink on Ecorse Road.

A sustaining and guiding force for fine community activities in the interest of our young people has been the Parent-Teachers' Association. Mrs. Ursula Benns, a resident since June, 1944, has been active in PTA work for more than ten years. When she moved into the Village her oldest child Douglas was eight years old; he is now a tall young man who attends Eastern Michigan College. Douglas and his oldest sister Diana, who was seven years old when the family moved in, entered Ross School, and Kathy, who was four years old, attended the War Day-Care Center at Simmonds School.

Judy Benns will be the first of the family to have obtained all of her schooling in the Willow Run schools, when she graduates from the new Willow Run High School in June, 1956, and Kathy will be the second when she graduates in 1957.

It was natural that Mrs. Benns, having five children, would be interested in the PTA. Even while working full time for the PHA Management Office and managing her home, she has served as President of the Ross PTA and as President of the Edmonson Junior High PTA, and has been a leader of girl scout troops.

"I think the Willow Run PTA has done an exceptional job," Mrs. Benns said, "when you consider the problem of families constantly moving out and moving in. For several years there was an average of a hundred families a month who moved out and a hundred families a month who moved in. In a year's time, that represents nearly one-half of our total families."

"What are some of the things you recall that the PTA has done?" I asked.

"One year the PTA volunteered to help with the lunch program to give the teachers some relief. We had the Thrift Shop which sold donated used clothing. Funds raised through the Thrift Shop were used for worthy causes, such as sponsoring Boy Scout troops and Girl Scout troops."

"Despite the constant turnover of the population, do you feel that the PTA has helped to give the residents the feeling of belonging?" I asked.

"I most certainly do," Mrs. Benns replied. "A family does not have to be in the Village very long to realize that there is no problem of 'keeping up with the Joneses.' Most Village families try to be good neighbors. Since most of our families have children, the children help the parents to get acquainted. Children are not bound by the formalities of being introduced. When they live on the same street and go to the same school with other children, they get the parents acquainted in a hurry."

"Do you think," I asked, "that your children have had as good educational advantages as children in nearby communities?"

"I think our children have had better educational advantages at Willow Run than in many communities. I will give you an example. One of my youngsters had a reading problem. Through the work of the visiting teacher this child had the opportunity for special help in remedial reading. She is now a good reader. There are not many school systems where this problem would have been discovered and corrected at such an early stage.

"Have any of our children ever had to be on half-day sessions? The answer is 'No.' All of our children have had regular full-day schedules. There are not many communities which can boast of such a record," said Mrs. Benns.

"In addition to the good program of our schools and the work of the PTA," I asked, "do you think there are any other advantages in raising a family in the Village?"

"The Village," Mrs. Benns told me, "is like a nice small town. People are friendly and learn soon to be good neighbors. Good neighbors are co-operative and willing to help each other in case of emergency. I feel fortunate that my children had the opportunity to grow up in a community like Willow Run."

Foster School

Children Registering at Foster School

VILLAGE SCHOOL SYSTEM

11

Dr. Malcolm Rogers was employed as the first Superintendent of Schools for Willow Run in July, 1943, when it was in the process of making a sudden and dramatic change from a one-building school district to a full-fledged school system. When Dr. Rogers came here, the only school in the district was Spencer, but the three others, Foster, Ross, and Simmonds, were under construction.

Starting a new school system had advantages. There was the challenge of planning a curriculum around the most modern educational concepts, and the challenge of recruiting and employing teachers who saw the great possibilities in a new system. There were no previously established traditions to combat.

But, starting a new school system also had its disadvantages, especially in wartime. There was a myriad of problems. Mrs. Dorothy Lindquist, who was Dr. Rogers' first secretary, told me about some of them.

"Our first office was in Spencer School, because the other schools were still under construction when the fall term opened in 1943. All of the children in the district were registered at Spencer. By the middle of September, Foster School was opened, so we moved our office to that building and remained there until Simmonds opened in November. We then moved to that building. The day we moved into our office at Foster, we found that the next room was the carpenters' headquarters. On the day the children reported, the workmen were still hanging doors and windows and painting the walls. The furniture was still in crates and stacked in the halls and rooms."

"How could you start a school," I asked, "with no chairs to sit on?"

"Everyone pitched in," she said. "Children, teachers, office workers, all unpacked furniture, arranged it, and swept the floors. Some of the youngsters suggested to the painters the colors they would like for the walls."

bert Stevenson, Principal, Welcomes the Boys and Girls
Foster School on Opening Day, 1950

"What about teaching supplies?" I asked. "Did the teachers have the necessary books, pencils, paper, charts, and maps?"

Mrs. Lindquist replied that "supplies had been ordered, but due to the shortage of so many items and the priorities of the war agencies, many teachers taught children for weeks without any actual teaching supplies."

Mrs. Lindquist laughed as she told us the problem of pencil sharpeners. "Pencil sharpeners were not to be found. We finally discovered one dealer that did have a limited supply of parts for pencil sharpeners so that old ones could be repaired. We kept buying different parts until we got enough to assemble one pencil sharpener for each building. We certainly needed more than one to a building but we managed that first year."

Mrs. Lindquist also told us that Dr. Rogers was never certain during that first year whether there would be funds available to meet each payroll. All Michigan school districts receive funds known as State Aid. This money is allocated to each district on the basis of the number of children in the district at the time of the school census, which is taken in May of each year. In May, 1943, there were 335 school children in the district. The State Aid for the term, beginning in September, was based on that number of children, but before the end of that school year, more than 2,000 children had been registered in the schools.

In addition to State Aid, school districts derive their income from local real estate taxes, and, in special situations, from the United States Office of Education. Federal property is usually tax free; however, the government realized that in the case of federal housing projects, it had an obligation toward local community services such as education. The Lanham Act, the legislation which authorized the building of temporary government housing, provided that money should be paid to all local taxing bodies that would be comparable to amounts paid on a regular tax assessment; so additional federal funds, distributed through the United States Office of Education, were made available to those school districts which experienced an increase in school enrollment due to the influx of war workers and their families.

Despite the availability of these sources of funds for school operation, there was the problem of getting the money into the school bank account. "Dr. Rogers had to do a lot of telephoning, letter writing, and knocking on doors," Mrs. Lindquist said. "Somehow he managed to keep enough money coming in to meet each payroll, although there were several times we were never sure until the last day."

To meet the needs of those families in which both parents worked at the plant, one Day-Care Center for preschool children was opened at Foster School in October, 1943, and in February a second was opened at Simmonds School. These centers provided care for little children from 6 A.M. to 6 P.M. each day. Also, since working parents did not arrive home until late afternoon, a program was arranged to take care of school-age children after school.

With the assistance of the University of Michigan, the Willow Run Library was started in 1944. Books were collected from schools in Ann Arbor and donated to Willow Run. Later, funds were made available to purchase new books to expand the library.

Alfred "Pete" Brose, with the financial help of Lanham funds, established a community-wide program of recreation and adult education.

He is especially proud of the intramural athletic program which was organized. Beginning with the fourth grade, each room had teams in baseball, softball, and basketball. Regular games were scheduled between the different schools. "It is no wonder," Pete said, "that Willow Run made such a fine showing its first year in interscholastic athletics. Those boys had an early start in athletic competition."

Prior to the sudden expansion of the school district in 1943, only a kindergarten through sixth-grade program was offered. The rest of the children attended school in Ypsilanti, but with the increase in population in the summer of 1943, the facilities of the schools in Ypsilanti became so heavily taxed that they could no longer provide educational services for the Willow Run boys and girls. To meet this problem, the Willow Run schools expanded their program to include the eighth grade. Students in the ninth grade were taken by bus to schools in Ypsilanti.

Who were the boys and girls who attended our schools during the war years? They came from many places, from varied educational and cultural backgrounds. They came from 849 towns in 36 states and from Canada. These boys and girls

Willow Run Basketball Champs, Foster School, 1946

reflected the sentiments of their parents—they felt that they were temporary residents of a temporary community. "Home" was another town, another state, to which they and their parents would return as soon as the war ended. The feeling of being "temporary," of having no roots in the place in which one lives, affects the attitudes of boys and girls.

Miss Sarah King, the first music teacher at Foster School, had taught some children the words to well-known national songs, like "America," "The Star-Spangled Banner," "My Old Kentucky Home," and "Dixie." She then taught them the words to the song, "Michigan, My Michigan." Mr. Stevenson, another member of the staff, visited the class the day the children were to sing these songs.

"They sang all of the songs very nicely," Mr. Stevenson told me. "They seemed to thoroughly enjoy their singing until they came to that last song, 'Michigan, My Michigan.' Most of them just stopped singing. Miss King encouraged them but they were indifferent." He explained that most of them felt it was not "their Michigan." They were expressing their feeling of being temporary residents in a temporary community. Michigan belonged to other people, not to them.

By the end of 1945, many of these children had returned with their parents to

Willow Run High School Band

specting the New Edmonson Elementary School

their own homes. With the end of the war and the return of veterans, many new families moved to Willow Run. Our school leaders worked and planned to meet the needs of the postwar community. As a result of a study made in 1946, the school board, parents, and students voted in favor of the institution of a junior high school. It was established in September, 1947, and was located in Ross School.

As more and more children reached school age, our school board was faced with the problem of providing additional facilities. Negotiations were begun in 1949 to obtain West Lodge from the government and in September, 1950, it was renovated and opened as an intermediate school. In 1951, land was secured and plans drawn for the new Edmonson School, which was opened in the fall of 1952. It provided a junior high school for the entire school district as well as a wing for the elementary children in the immediate area. Our school board continued to plan for the future so that, in the fall of 1955, the Willow Run High School on Spencer Road was opened. In the senior class which will graduate in June, 1956, there are sixteen boys and girls who have received all of their schooling at Willow Run.

During the war years of 1943–44, a total of 2,195 pupils was registered in our schools. By May, 1944, the number of students remaining in the district was 1,706.

Edmonson Junior High School Girls Put On a Style Show

This number decreased to 1,406 in May, 1945, the year that many of the Village families left for their home communities because of the discontinuation of the production of bombers.

With the opening of the Village to returning veterans and their families, school enrollment gradually began to increase each year, so that in May, 1955, there were 3,833 boys and girls attending our six elementary, junior high, and senior high schools.

While our school board and administrators have tried continually to meet the needs for school facilities, our teachers, principals, and administrators have worked

Edmonson Junior High School Library Helpers, Mrs. Nell Barrett, Head Librarian

diligently to improve the educational standards of our schools. This has been a difficult and challenging task, since, during each school year, there are hundreds of children who move away, and hundreds of others who come from other areas. to enroll.

Board members Glenn Spencer, Robert Cowling, and Andrew Grenier have each given years of conscientious service to the children in Willow Run Village. They and their predecessors have set a high standard of achievement. Along with the newer board members, Richard Branham and Lonnie Maynor, they are continuing to work for the best educational standards possible.

Principals and Teachers Meet to Plan Improved Standards

It is little wonder that the school district was recently selected as a "Lighthouse" School District. This is an honorary title given to those exceptional schools which are outstanding in the progress and quality of their educational program. Willow Run can be proud of the results of the hard work and educational pioneering by its school leaders.

SCHOOL BOARD REPRESENTATION

12

Members of the Resident Council came to realize that of all the forces in the community which had a direct bearing on all of the people, next to the management, the most important unit of government was the public school. Our Willow Run school district is officially known as School District Number 1, Fractional, Ypsilanti Township, Willow Run, Michigan. The word "fractional" is used because the district lies in two townships, that part of the Village in Superior Township being included in this school district. The Willow Run district includes all of the Village, plus an area south of Holmes Road, across Michigan Avenue, and including a portion of the Bomber Plant. The district extends to Ford Lake, east of Harris Road to the extension of Dorset Street. It extends eastward to the Expressway and to a portion of Rawsonville Road.

There is a state law making it mandatory that any person, to be eligible for election to a school board in Michigan, must own property. This meant that, in 1948, the members of the school board were all property owners living in that section of the school district which is outside the Village, even though over 75 per cent of the children registered in the Willow Run Public Schools were residents of the Village. The Resident Council did not think it fair that the Village was not represented on the school board, so the council organized a group of interested residents into a "Better Schools Committee."

I talked to Mrs. Mary McCarthy of Ypsilanti about the problems. She was a member of the Resident Council and served on the Better Schools Committee. She and her husband Gerald lived at that time with their children on Goshen Court.

"There was the possibility of trying to get the State Legislature to change the law so that non-property owners could run for school board election," she said, "but

Willow Run Board of Education and Administrators—SEATED: *Andrew Grenier, Treasurer; Lonnie Maynor, Trustee; Robert Cowling, Trustee; Glen Spencer, President; Richard Branham, Secretary.* STANDING: *Albert Johnsen, Superintendent; Robert Stevenson, Assistant Superintendent; Alcuin Wiench, Business Manager*

there was every possibility that the law would never be changed. We wanted to do something right at the moment. We studied all possible angles within existing law to figure out what to do to get fair representation."

What the Better Schools Committee of the Council did to get fair representation on the school board makes one realize that a great many things are possible under existing laws, if a study is made to find the way.

"At one of our meetings, Betty Tableman told us that a group of teachers in the Dearborn school system jointly owned a piece of property in Dearborn so that all of them would be eligible to vote on school bond issues in school elections." Mary McCarthy's keen eyes danced as she told us the rest of the story.

"I contacted a real estate broker and told him about our problem. I explained that we wanted to purchase a piece of property located within the school district. I also explained that we did not have very much money, so we would need an inexpensive lot.

"The broker located a lot on East Grand Boulevard. It could not be used for building purposes since it was so swampy. He arranged with the owner to sell us the lot for two hundred dollars with the agreement that we would not sell the lot to any other purchaser without giving the original owner first option to buy it back."

"How did you decide," I asked, "who should be the buyers of the lot?"

"We had agreed on a slate of Village candidates to run for the board," Mary replied. "The original purchasers of the lot were three Village couples: Gerald and myself, Mr. and Mrs. Robert Cowling, and Mr. and Mrs. Burleson Fitzharris. Our slate of candidates was Bob Cowling, Burleson Fitzharris, and Gerald McCarthy."

It was not enough, however, to get a slate of candidates who lived in Willow Run Village and were property owners. Village residents had paid little attention to school board elections as long as none of their neighbors or acquaintances were eligible. The council members who were concerned with the school problem worked long and late. They organized committees by courts and areas. Night after night these hard-working residents of Willow Run rapped on doors.

"Are you registered to vote in the school elections?" they would ask. (At that time, to be eligible to vote in a school election, the voter had to be registered with the schools. Since then, a change has been made whereby a voter who is registered with his township clerk for the general elections may vote in all elections including school elections.) If the answer to the constantly repeated question was one of doubt, the council member made an appointment with the resident to take him over to the school board office to register.

"But I cannot leave the house," some residents said, "I have no one to stay with the children."

"Never mind that," answered the caller. "Tell us when you will be ready to register and we will bring you a baby sitter."

"How much will it cost?" asked the residents.

*First Willow Run Housing Project Members on School Board Meet with Superin-
tendent and a Former Board Member: Ralph M. Van Volkinburg, Robert Cowling,
Leo Hosman, Burleson Fitzharris, Gerald McCarthy*

"This is a service which we are providing," answered the election worker. "There is no charge. We just want you to register."

Day after day the hard-working committee members took their cars and drove hundreds of potential voters to the school office to register to vote in the school elections, while the baby-sitter volunteers took care of the children.

In the previous school elections, the largest number of votes cast for any candidate had been less than a hundred. In June, 1949, the three candidates from Willow Run polled 496 to 557 votes each. This excellent voting record was the direct result of sound planning followed by constant hard work.

I asked Burleson Fitzharris how it felt to be one of the first Village residents to be elected to school board membership. "It was really exciting the night of that election," he said. "Some of the people who were at the meeting checking votes said it was not legal."

I asked him what they did to prove the legality of the election. "We had a lawyer with us," he said. "Our lawyer assured the doubters that we were elected legally. The people who doubted us contacted another lawyer who verified the legality of the election."

Mr. Fitzharris, although a local businessman at the time, had attended the University of Michigan. He had completed most of his work for a master's degree in public administration. He and his fellow candidates had studied the law very thoroughly as it applied to school elections. They had put this academic knowledge to sound practical use.

Ever since that famous school election in 1949, our Willow Run School Board has always had Village residents among its members.

In addition to the original three residents who were elected to the school board in 1949, the following Village residents have at some time served on the Board: Marvin Tableman, Dr. Victor Zerbi, Donald Bouton, Richard Branham, and Lonnie Maynor.

The deed to the swampy lot now has more than 200 names as owners. Many Village residents have had their names attached to that deed so that they would be eligible to vote on school bond issues.

One cannot help but wonder, when going down East Grand Boulevard in the early spring, if those dozens of croaking frogs are acclaiming their community landlord. Perhaps they are reminding us that their home made it possible for the families who have lived in Willow Run Village to have representation on the school board.

A GOOD PLACE IN WHICH TO LIVE

13

In 1946, the sign at the corner of Clark and Prospect Roads read "Willow Run Village—Temporary Veterans' Housing." There were similar signs on whatever route one took to get to Willow Run. But the word "temporary" did not bother the thousands of GI's and their families who came to live at Willow Run after 1945. The GI's had become accustomed to the variable meanings of the word "temporary." Some had been stationed at an army outpost on a temporary basis—which could mean anything from a few weeks to a few years.

The big concern of those GI veterans was "right now." This was the community in which they lived, and they wanted it to be a good one. The Public Housing Administration worked with these resident veterans to make Willow Run a good place in which to live.

Ken C. Cavanaugh became the Manager of Willow Run on September 1, 1947. This is what Mr. Cavanaugh considered his greatest challenge when he came to Willow Run: "With a temporary city, already at its physical life expectancy, and with over 12,000 residents from every social pattern desperately needing housing, my greatest challenge was to organize a maintenance staff that could hold the buildings together, and a tenant relations staff that could help the families properly understand the situation and live together until better housing was available."

Mr. Cavanaugh remained as Manager of Willow Run until late October, 1949. He organized a staff that, to a great extent, carried out the objectives for which he had hoped. Walter L. Funkhouser, who had been Assistant Manager, became Manager in 1951 and continued those policies, as did Paul Moore, who is the present Manager of Willow Run. Through all these years, every effort has been made to have a

Willow Village Resident Council — SEATED: *William Ross, Marvin Tableman, President, Donald Geise, Dayton Ford.* STANDING: *Jacques De Laurier, William Reading, John Tomasko, Jr.*

sound financial operation, but with a regard and respect for the people and their problems.

Unlike the usual town, city, or village, there was no local government. Willow Run Village was a government-owned housing project; the people who worked there to operate the project were employees of the United States Government. All of the residents living in the Village were tenants who paid rent to a landlord— the United States Government. Checks were made payable to the Treasurer of the United States.

Since there were no locally elected officials, no local government, no city council or township board to consult, a group of residents organized the first Resident Council. The council met with members of the management staff to discuss problems of residents, one of which was, council members felt, that the means of communication between management and residents was inadequate. The management staff had planned to publish a resident handbook which would be distributed to all residents, and this was exactly the sort of publication for which the council had hoped. At the request of the management staff, the council prepared the following statement which was included in the handbook.

The Willow Run Village Resident Council was formed early in 1947 to act for the residents in making this community a better place in which to live.

This Village-wide representative body is working for all the residents to further:
1. Effective management of the Village for the benefit of the residents.
2. Equal treatment of residents regardless of race, color or creed.
3. Enforcement of provisions for the protection of public health, welfare and safety.
4. Promotion of community awareness.
5. Resident participation, through the Resident Council, in the formulation of management policies vitally affecting the residents.

The **Resident Handbook** included the following statement prepared by the management staff:

Purpose of Handbook

The purpose of this handbook is to serve as a reference and guide to you, the residents of Willow Run Village. Frequent questions arise in your mind as to Management Policy, Maintenance Standards, and your own responsibilities. This handbook could not begin to answer all the detailed questions. It can give you general basic information. Questions not answered here should be referred to the Service Desk, Management Office.

Be assured that it is our aim to give you the best possible service within the limitations of our budgets and staff. Your understanding and co-operation will make our communal living here in the Village cordial and friendly. We suggest that you keep this booklet handy for easy reference.

You Should Expect from Management
1. Adequate maintenance and reasonable service for necessary repairs.
2. Courteous consideration of your requests for repairs and all matters pertaining to the comfort, safety and welfare of you and your family.
3. Co-operation and assistance in developing programs for the betterment of the community.
4. Fair and impartial treatment to all alike.

Management Should Expect from the Resident
1. Strict observance of the lease you have signed, which includes the "Terms and Conditions of Occupancy."
2. Proper care of your premises, inside and outside. Co-operation in keeping communal areas clean, neat, and attractive.
3. Consideration for your neighbors and for your community.
4. Careful observation of all rules and regulations now in effect or which may be adopted by Management.

Basic Points for Successful Living in a Public Housing Project
1. Pay your rent **on time**—on or before the first day of each month.
2. Read carefully the "Terms and Conditions of Occupancy."
3. Care for your dwelling as if you owned it. You are also a tax-payer.
4. Respect your neighbors' rights. Conduct yourself as you would have your neighbor conduct himself.

Early in 1948, the management staff began publication of the **Management Newsletter,** which was written and mailed once each month to every family in the Village. The purpose of the newsletter was to continue the means of communication between the Management Office and the residents which had been started with the **Handbook.** It attempted to keep the residents informed of current policies. It brought announcements and news regarding events and programs of special interest to residents, and encouraged residents to co-operate with management in making the Village a safe and healthy place to live—a community of which the people could be proud.

Members of the Resident Council and those of the housing staff co-operated to promote their mutual aims, whether they were precautions to prevent fires or the beautification of yard areas. Whenever there was a community-wide drive, such as the Red Feather Drive, Red Cross, or March of Dimes, the Resident Council assumed the responsibility of doing the job. On two occasions the Ypsilanti Community Chest presented the Resident Council the little Indian statue with his red feather, symbolizing a special award to the group in the greater community which had made the best record in the Community Chest Drive.

The Resident Council also assumed responsibility for the community gardens. There are several large areas within the Village that can be used for vegetable gardens. These garden areas are located behind Malden Court, between Springfield and Wiard Road, and in the loop between MacArthur and Stamford. The council has always arranged to have these areas plowed and disked, and council members have done the plot measuring and staking. Although these areas were on government property, the Management Office approved of the council charging a rental fee for use of these garden plots. The fee of $1.00 to $1.75, depending on the size of the plot, has covered the cost of plowing, disking, and staking. Some Village families saved a great deal of money on food bills because of their gardens, and many others spent happy hours just enjoying the work.

Despite the signs at the Village which read "Temporary," Willow Run Village was a community that had begun to mature. It happened because the residents who lived there wanted a good community, and because the landlord, the United States government, had a staff of people who worked hard to help make it a good community.

First-Prize Winner in Village Beautification Campa

126

TIME RUNS OUT

14

Willow Run Village was made possible because of federal legislation known as the Lanham Act, passed by Congress in October, 1940. From the time the Act was passed, the "disposition" of the housing was constantly in question. Housing had to be provided for the war worker and his family, but the federal government's role as landlord was not to be easily shed.

In 1943 Congress asked that war housing disposition be completed within two years after the end of the national emergency. In 1945, after V-E Day, Title V was added to the Lanham Act, allowing the transfer of temporary housing units from war use to veterans' use.

In 1947 Congress began to draft firm deadlines for the disposition of temporary housing projects throughout the United States. It was agreed that temporary veterans' housing could be transferred to local communities with the stipulation that the units could not be resold as housing, but must be publicly operated.

With the start of the Korean conflict in the spring of 1950, the deadline for the disposition of temporary veterans' housing, which included Willow Run, was suspended. However, there was the awareness that the Village could not go on indefinitely as a temporary community. A group of residents of Willow Run organized the Willow Run Re-Development Committee in 1950. The original members of this group were all active in community affairs. Among them were: Marvin Tableman and his wife Betty; Mr. Tableman had received his Ph.D. degree in political science at the University of Michigan and was an instructor there. He was president of the Resident Council at that time. Gerald McCarthy was an office employee at the Kaiser-Frazer plant and served on the school board. Mrs. Shirley Ackenhusen was president of the Ross School PTA and Executive Secretary of the Co-op Committee. Jacques DeLaurier taught at Ross School, was active in the Resident Council, and was chairman of the County Welfare Committee. Robert Cowling was Justice of the Peace and a member of the school board. Reverend Edwards, minister of the United Church Federation, was a trustee on the Board of the Community Chest in Ypsilanti. Burleson M. Fitzharris was a member of the school board and a local businessman. These and other Willow Run community leaders formed the nucleus of the Willow Run Re-Development Committee. They were also the charter members of the Willow Run Co-operative Association. This group felt that nothing was being done to meet the housing needs of the residents of Willow Run Village in the event that the buildings were to be torn down. No one seemed to be considering where people were to live. The only problem seemed to be the disposition of the federal land. The committee attempted to have mass meetings and arouse the interest of the residents, but they had no definite plan of action. The meetings dwindled from two hundred and fifty supporters to the original group, which then proceeded to function without community-wide support.

They conferred with land-planners and obtained legal counsel. At that time, neither the Ypsilanti Township Board nor the Superior Township Board felt that they could afford to purchase the utilities. It seemed to the committee that the only recourse which they had, to plan an orderly redevelopment of the area, was to incorporate. To have an adequate tax base, the incorporation would have to include the entire school district, with the former .Bomber Plant which was then being operated by the Kaiser-Frazer Corporation.

After several meetings at which there were heated discussions, the committee decided that before proceeding with incorporation, the City of Ypsilanti should be consulted on the possibility of annexing the area involved. This necessitated a majority approval by the voters in the City of Ypsilanti, the voters in the Village, and the voters in that strip of property in the township which lies between the City and the Village. But before the issue could be put to a vote of the people, an injunction was filed by one of the property owners in the township which temporarily stopped efforts to go forward with either plans for annexation to Ypsilanti or incorporation of the Village and adjacent area.

In June, 1951, the Manager of Willow Run, Walter Funkhouser, was notified of a "vacancy freeze" to be effective the first day of July. This notice came from the Central Office of the PHA in Washington, D. C. The notice was an explanation of Section 604 of the Lanham Act, as amended by Congress.

What did the vacancy freeze mean? It meant that after July, 1951, no new tenants could move into vacated apartments in the Village. The notice, however, also stated that exceptions could be made to this order. One exception depended upon the total population of a housing project as compared to the total population of the municipality in which it was situated, as recorded in the 1940 census. If the population of the housing project exceeded 30 per cent of the population of the municipality, the order would not apply.

Willow Run Village was not located in a municipality; it was located outside the limits of the City of Ypsilanti. The northern half of Willow Run was in Superior Township, and the southern half in Ypsilanti Township. The township dividing line was the old Clark Road. (Clark Road below Swansea Court curves south. The old Clark Road did not curve south, but ran due east and west). This meant that the township line cut through the middle of Sudbury Court, part of Norfolk Court, and through Enfield Court.

Since Willow Run was not in a municipality, the question arose as to whether or not the Village would be exempt from the order. The population of the Village exceeded by far the population of the two townships as revealed in the 1940 census.

The **Michigan Daily,** a newspaper published by the students at the University of Michigan in Ann Arbor, on July 4, 1951, published the following story:

VILLAGE RENTAL OFFICES STILL FILL VACANCIES. The Willow Run Rental Office is continuing to fill vacancies in the midst of legal confusion and conflicting rumor from "usually reliable" sources about its actual status.

Walter L. Funkhouser, general housing manager of the Village, filled vacancies Monday on the basis of a report that an order had been issued from Washington declaring the Village exempt under the "municipality" clause of the Federal Housing Act of 1950.

Saturday, however, President Truman signed a stop-gap bill extending, for 45 days, the life of the Lanham Act of 1948, the original temporary housing measure under which Willow Village was constructed. . . .

Other sources feel the extension definitely applies to the Village. Marvin Tableman, president of the Resident Council . . . received a wire from Michigan Senator Moody, that Tableman interpreted as implying the extension did extend the life of the Village.

Mr. Funkhouser was eventually notified that Willow Run Village was exempt under the municipality clause. Many people sighed with relief. The Village had a stay of execution. There was a little more time—maybe something would happen. Vacant apartments were being rented to new tenants, and living in the Village would go on. The question was, "How long?"

In the meantime, many of the active community leaders moved away from Willow Run. Marvin Tableman was appointed an Assistant to Governor Williams, so he and his wife moved to Lansing. Jacques DeLaurier was selected to be an Administrative Assistant to the late Senator Blair Moody, and the DeLauriers moved to Washington, D. C. Reverend Edwards and his family moved east to a fine new pastorate. The McCarthys were anxious to own their own home, so they found a house that they liked and moved to Ypsilanti. With the expansion of his business interests into Ypsilanti, Mr. Fitzharris and his family purchased a home and moved to that city.

New residents took over the leadership in the Village. They met, they conferred, they planned. But the sands of time were running out. In August, 1953, Mr. Funkhouser, the Village Manager, met with officials of both the Ypsilanti Township Board and the Superior Township Board to discuss the need of a resolution by Superior Township.

Ypsilanti Township, under provisions of the Lanham Act, had filed an application with the PHA to acquire the Village. Since half of the buildings were located in Superior Township, a waiver from Superior Township was necessary to permit Ypsilanti Township to acquire the total Village.

For more than a year, nothing was decided, nothing was settled. The people who worked and lived at Willow Run did not know from day to day when the end of the Village would come.

On October 6, 1954, Paul Moore, who had been appointed Manager of the Village when Mr. Funkhouser transferred to Norfolk, Virginia, received a telegram from the Chicago Field Office of the PHA notifying him to freeze vacancies and get ready to dispose of the project within six months if no agreement was reached between the two townships within five days. On that same day, all of the government employees at Willow Run received notice that their employment with the government would be terminated at the end of thirty days.

That evening the **Ypsilanti Press** carried a headline story telling of the end of Willow Run Village within six months. Albert Johnsen, Superintendent of the Willow Run schools, called the Management Office. "What does this mean?" he asked. "Is it really true that all of the residents will be given a six months' eviction notice?"

The office told Mr. Johnsen that it was true. He was told that the only hope for any extended life of the Village hinged on acquisition of the Village by Ypsilanti Township.

"How can we do any adequate planning for our schools if this happens?" he asked.

"You probably can't," was the answer.

On the evening of October 8, 1954, the boards of both townships met to try and solve the problem. The discussion continued until midnight. Both township boards then recessed to discuss their individual problems in relation to the Village. When they reconvened, Superior Township announced that its members would sign the waiver.

"What did you do with that form?" Mr. Ehle, Ypsilanti Township Clerk, asked Mr. Hicks, the Township Supervisor.

"I don't have it. You must have filed it," Mr. Hicks answered.

After a hurried search in desks and files, the much discussed waiver form was located. The PHA representative was not sure how many copies of the form would be needed but suggested that three would be enough. Since only one copy had been located, Mr. Ehle adjourned to his office and typed out the additional copies.

Somehow the time taken to search for the lost waiver form and to type the

fficials Sign Documents Transferring Willow Run Village
rom U.S. to Ypsilanti Township, October 30, 1954

additional copies seemed to relieve the tensions that had developed with the hours of discussion. The people at that meeting started to smile, to relax, to talk about other things.

During the next three weeks the township officials and the PHA officials worked diligently to complete the myriad legal details necessary for the transfer of the Village from United States government ownership to local township ownership.

The **Ypsilanti Press** of October 29, 1954, carried a banner headline story:

YPSILANTI TOWNSHIP BUYS WILLOW VILLAGE
First steps toward transforming Willow Run, famous "Bomber City" of World War II, from a war relic to a permanent community, were taken today when officials of the Federal government and Ypsilanti Township signed documents closing sale of part of the huge sprawling project and optioning the remainder of the Township.

While other officials looked on in the historic moments, Supervisor Henry F. Hicks and Township Clerk Don Ehle for Ypsilanti Township, and Hugo C. Schwartz, Assistant Director for Disposition in the Chicago Field Office of the Public Housing Administration, acting for the Government, signed deeds, mortgages and option agreements.

The simple signing ceremony took place at 10 o'clock this morning in the Township Hall just outside the city of Ypsilanti. Attending were members of the Ypsilanti and Superior Township Boards.

Sold to the Township are 537 acres of land on which are located 3,003 dwelling units, the remainder of more than 8,200 which at the peak of their occupancy, housed nearly 20,000 persons. Also in the sale are four vacant parcels totaling 139 acres on which Township officials anticipate construction of new homes will start in the near future.

Optioned to the Township today are vacant areas totaling 965 acres and the business district. The options expire in six months and if not taken up by the Township, the properties covered by them will be offered to other purchasers by the government. Included in the commercial area are a 1,200 seat theatre, two filling stations, a drug store, three grocery stores, a general store, barber shop and beauty parlor, and other small shops and services.

The Public Housing Administration is giving the Township dwelling units without other consideration than that the Township assume responsibility to remove them from the site. Michigan law requires removal to be completed by June 30, 1958. Sale of the land is on the basis of the acquisition cost to the government with the Township to pay approximately $325,000 for the dwellings site and the four vacant parcels being taken now . . .

The Township expects to meet its obligations out of rentals from the dwellings and sale of vacant areas. . . .

Relinquishment by the Public Housing Administration to the Township of this community of approximately 11,000 people is in accordance with an amendment to the Lanham Act under which it was built, authorizing PHA to make disposition of temporary war projects to local governing bodies who certify to a continuing need for the housing and agree to demolish the structures when the need has ended.

The Ypsilanti Township Board made application for relinquishment under terms of the Act by June 30, 1953, but the project was not declared surplus by the government until January of this year.

"Our immediate purpose in taking over the dwelling areas of the project," Supervisor Hicks said for the Township Board, "is to keep from having nearly 2,500 families evicted by the Public Housing Administration, which had no choice but to tear down the houses and sell the land if we did not take over. A census of the project families for school purposes, taken last spring, showed that nearly 7,000 men and women from Willow Run families were then employed. I understand that there has been a little decline from that level. That is a big payroll and of great economic importance in this area.

"To save that buying power for this area, we had to act to maintain the present dwellings until new ones could be supplied, since there was no place for the families to go if the PHA had to evict for demolition. If we did not do what we are doing, we would have a situation similar to what we had when the Bomber Plant was built without adequate housing being built with it.

"Our long range plan is to have the area redeveloped by private builders as fast as it can be done. With the property under our control we can see that it is properly handled with sound planning and good construction. . . ."

"Mr. Hicks and his associates on the Board are to be commended for taking bold action to save the families of Willow Run from hardship and for planning for the future," Mr. Schwartz said. "Had they not taken over the project, we would have been compelled to evict the families early next year after having given them six months' notice. We have been glad to co-operate with the Township and feel that the interests of the government and this area have both been well served by the relinquishment of the project to the Township."

Willow Run Airport and Terminal, Plant in Foreground

Willow Run was truly the "Bomber City" of the war and was as much an adjunct of the great Bomber Plant, operated by the Ford Company, as any of the stamping machines in the factory or the huge airport at its doors. The plant itself was one of the great wonders of the American production genius, turning out a total of approximately 8,600 of the famous B-24's. The plant backed the invasion of Europe by our armed forces with a bomber an hour rolling from its three quarters of a mile of assembly lines.

Like the huge Bomber Plant, which has become an economic asset to the area, Willow Run is being preserved for the ways of peace.

APPENDIX

THE FINANCING OF
WILLOW RUN VILLAGE

The United States government spent approximately 20 million dollars to build Willow Run Village. This money purchased 2,064 acres of land, provided for the site improvements including roads and streets, and built 30 dormitory buildings with 3,860 rooms. Nine hundred and sixty trailers with laundry and toilet facilities were installed. Temporary row housing with 3,500 apartments, six community buildings of which three had cafeterias, a management office, an infirmary, a movie theatre, police and fire stations, maintenance buildings and commercial buildings for stores, and filling stations were built. The water department with its deep wells, the sewage disposal plant, and the first three schools were financed and built by the Federal Works Agency with its war emergency funds.

The average cost of operating the Village was one million dollars a year. This money paid the wages of the people required to do the office and maintenance work, bought the necessary supplies and materials to keep the buildings in repair, paid for the electricity, maintained the thirty miles of streets and roads, operated the water department, sewage disposal plant, and fire department, and made payments as taxes to the local political units of government.

The United States government stipulates that no local taxes shall be paid on federally owned property and buildings. In the case of public housing, the government agreed to make such payments to the local governing bodies at the current assessed valuation, to assure that the people who lived on such projects would obtain the same public services as the people who lived on privately owned property. These payments made to the local taxing bodies are known as payments in lieu of taxes.

Beginning July 1, 1943, through the end of 1954, a total of $965,697.51 was paid by the federal government to the local taxing units of government. The local units of government which received payments were the Willow Run and Ypsilanti school districts, Washtenaw County, and Ypsilanti and Superior townships. The Willow Run School District received the largest portion of this money, $713,890 for the twelve-year period.

Although it cost approximately one million dollars each year to operate the Village, the income received from the Village in rents paid by residents and lease-holders of the commercial areas exceeded this amount. Over the years, an average of $75,000 per year could be considered as profit which was returned to the Treasury of the United States.

Willow Run Actual Operating Budget July 1, 1952, through June 30, 1953

	Total	Per Unit-month*
Income	$1,136,904	$31.49
Net Income to U. S.	87,901	2.43
Operating Expense	1,049,003	29.06
Repairs and Maintenance	424,469	11.76
Electricity	174,762	4.84
Other utilities	57,515	1.59
Management	124,244	3.44
Taxes	112,587	3.12
Operating Services (sanitation, streets and roads, public safety, other)	155,426	4.31

* Unit-month is the average amount of money for each apartment, each month.

Summary of Payment in Lieu of Taxes

Local Taxing Body	Payment
Willow Run School District (July 1, 1943 through June 30, 1955)	$713,890.00
Ypsilanti City School District (July 1, 1943 through June 30, 1955)	11,274.75
County of Washtenaw (January 1, 1944 through Dec. 31, 1955)	223,467.68
Ypsilanti Township (April 1, 1943 through March 31, 1950)	9,404.81
Superior Township (April 1, 1943 through March 31, 1950)	7,660.27
Total	$965,697.51